Conquering College

What colleges are really looking for,

how to write a stellar application,

and must-know college survival tips

Austin Fadely

Dedication

To my wife, Melanie, whose support and inspiration I could not do without; to my daughters, Kayla, Emma, and Clara, whose futures are in my hands; to my parents, Tyler and Linda, who taught me to trust in myself; to my sister, Grace, whose thoughtful questions inspired me to write this book, and to the teachers and professors, who tirelessly strive to realize the potential of us all.

Table of Contents

Foreword

For high school students, Conquering College defines successful strategies for getting into choice schools and thriving there. What sets this book apart is that it offers practical, proven tips from application to graduation.

When I started this book, I set out to cover absolutely everything I could think an aspiring high school student would need to know. I wanted to include all the tricks I learned, all the pitfalls to avoid, SAT sample problems, study tips, creative writing frameworks, and more. I didn't want to rely on my experience alone, so I spoke with high school students, teachers, and admissions counselors, anyone that had something useful to say about college. I read the top-sellers on the subject, too. I quickly came to realize I couldn't adequately cover everything I wanted in one book.

Instead, I focused on the essentials. I imagined what it would have been like if I had read something like this when I was in high school. There was so much that I didn't know then. After speaking with so many different people, I came to realize my experience wasn't unique. I realized the immediate thing on any senior's mind was the college application. The students I spoke with had tons of great questions, but they weren't sure how to get answers. So I took the next step. I started calling and emailing colleges across the country. I called small schools, big schools, East Coast, West Coast, etc. What I found out was enlightening.

The next thing I realized was that a lot of students don't know what to do once they get in. College is a different environment than high school, filled with greater responsibilities and distractions. There are fewer assignments, and grades have a bigger impact because there are fewer of them. The pace is often break-neck, and many college freshmen get derailed just trying to adjust.

I wanted to create something useful yet unique. There are plenty of books about applying to college, but none of them take it a step further. What do you need to know to succeed in college? I knew I had to go beyond the obvious and provide a pragmatic but effective guide—not just study tips and memorization techniques, but time and money management, finding jobs and internships, and setting goals and being accountable to them.

Part I of this book will demystify the application process, step through each section of the application, and provide tips on how to make your application better. I share the same writing process framework I use to approach all the formal essay-style writing I do.

Part II includes real-life skills that every college student should know, like where to find money to pay for school, how to stay afloat in a new environment, and useful tactics for studying, time and money management, how to build credit, and more.

My deepest hope is that this book empowers eager students and gives them the tools they need to truly conquer college.

-Austin Fadely

PART 1: GETTING ADMITTED

Applying to college is an exciting, stressful, and confusing time for a lot of students. You have a lot to manage already with classes and other activities. Fitting in the time for college applications is a challenge, but a necessary one.

First, we'll look at some things you should consider when picking your school. College isn't just about prestige or cost: it's about fit. Every university has a culture that permeates everything it does, right down to how it chooses its students. Pick a school where you fit in, and I guarantee you'll have a wonderful four years.

After that, I'll share some great advice I got from schools across the country. Many of the people I interviewed were Deans and Directors of Admissions. The schools vary in size and location, and you've probably heard of several on the list. Then we'll look at all the parts of the application, and highlight the most important aspects.

Finally, I'll walk you through the same writing process I used to create A-papers in college. We'll cover a lot of information, but by the end of it all, you'll be equipped to take on the college application.

Chapter 1

Looking Beyond High School

If you're reading this, chances are you're one of many students anxiously awaiting your chance to strike out on your own and make something of yourself. College is a big decision, but I've seen grad after grad rush into a decision without being fully informed or prepared.

This book will guide you through one of the bigger decisions of your life (though certainly not the biggest)! You undoubtedly have a ton of questions about what to do, what to expect, and how to get in.

Through the next several chapters, I'm going to provide you the tools to succeed wherever you choose to go. You'll learn about the admissions process and how best to approach it. You'll also learn a few key skills that will help you achieve success in college. By the end of this book, you will have a firmer grasp on what lies ahead of you in the coming years.

The Big Choice

Approaching senior year, thousands of high school students wrestle with the same questions. I've had the opportunity to see my sister and cousins work through the same issues I did when I was their age. It's a little funny looking back knowing what I know now and thinking there were some things I should have done differently. One thing I didn't understand was just how many different options are out there.

For me, I always assumed I would go to college. It's a straightforward formula right?

Good grades = good school = good job

Graduating during the spiral of the Great Recession, I realized there was much more to this formula than I thought. Sure, getting good grades would help you get into a good school, but that wasn't enough on its own. Having a college degree also didn't guarantee a job. I had to get out there and make my education work for me.

If you take nothing else from this book, know that nothing is handed to you. Although it's absolutely true that college graduates make more money over time on average than non-graduates, you have to be a little strategic about your education to see a big payoff. One thing you should consider is that we're talking about college graduates, which doesn't mean you have to go into a 4-year University right away.

There are many paths to a degree. You might decide to take two years at community college to save money and stay close to home at first. You might want to take a gap year and go traveling, or maybe you've decided to work for a year and save the money for college. None of these paths are better or worse. Each offers its strengths. Let's lay out a few different options:

Go to a 4-year University Right Away

This is a popular choice among students, and it's exactly what I did. I applied for and got accepted to the University of Maryland: Baltimore County. At the time, I didn't really know what I wanted to do, but I'd heard that it was more important to have a degree since most people don't work in fields they majored in (this is more baseless dogma than actual fact). Besides, the important thing to me was the experience of going to college and being on my own.

I was fortunate enough to receive a few scholarships and grants, which defrayed the cost a little. Even so, I ultimately took out loans to cover the difference. I came out owing around $24K for 3 ½ years of attendance, but those prices have gone up dramatically since I graduated, which wasn't all that long ago.

Okay, now let's put some numbers to this. We're going to figure out how much it can cost you. The National Center for Education Statistics has a helpful table you can see on their site.[1] All we need to know is that the annual cost of attending a public 4-year University is $16,789. (It's interesting to note that there is a 43% increase in the cost of attending

---

[1] http://nces.ed.gov/fastfacts/display.asp?id=76

such a school, and that doesn't even include currency inflation!)

Ok, so $16,789 x 4 years = $67,156 for a Bachelor's Degree.

Now, let's say 25% ($16,789) of that gets paid for, either through scholarships, grants, or help from your family. That means you have to take out a loan for $50,367.

Okay, $50K is up there, but it doesn't seem too bad right? Well, we haven't added in interest rates yet. An article from Bloomberg (*Student Loan Interest Rates Rise for 2015-2015 School Year*) puts interest rates at 4.66%. Let's round that to 4.5%.

If you get a federal subsidized loan, interest won't start accruing until you begin repayment (6 months after graduation). This is a generous assumption since only some loans will do that and usually only a portion of those loans don't accumulate interest while you're in school. Anyway, you have 10 years to pay off the loan, which means 120 payments.

Principal owed	$50,367
Annual rate	4.5%
Repayment period	10 years
Number of payments	120
Monthly payments	$522
Total paid over life of the loan	$62,639.47

This is the expected average to attend a public 4-year university for 4 years. If you didn't have any financial help that would total to $83,519.29 paid in student loans over 10 years.

2 Years Community College, 2 Years at University

If times are tough and money is tight, you may be considering going to community college for two years and transferring to a four-year university afterward. That's a great way to go and definitely something to consider. For one thing, you can stay local, cut down on costs for tuition, and you can probably stay with your folks and spend less for room and board than you would if you were living on campus. Most state schools will accept credit from most community colleges in the state, and a lot of CCs have feeder programs where you spend the first two years getting your general credits out of the way. After that, you transfer into the bigger state school once you're ready for your major.

If you have a big school in mind, especially an out-of-state one, check with their registrar to see if they will accept transfer credits from your local community college before you make a decision; otherwise, you'll have to go somewhere else, or you've spent two years wasting credits and money.

The trade off to going local is that you "miss out" on the big college experience, which is unfair. Yes, you'll miss out on the freshman experience of dirty roommates, smelly bathrooms, high-fat foods, and late night distractions from your work. You'll also miss out on the soul-crushing debt from your student loans after you graduate. Damn.

Looking back to our nces.ed.gov data, the annual cost of going to a 2-year college is $8,561. That's almost half annually!

Ok, so $8,561 x 2 years + $16,789 x 2 years = $50,700. That's $16,456 less than going to a University for all four years (more than that when you consider interest from student loans). Let's say you get the same financial help as before, $16,789. Now you're down to $33,911 in student loans.

Principal owed	$33,911
Annual rate	4.5%
Repayment period	10 years
Number of payments	120
Monthly payments	$351.45
Total paid over life of the loan	$42,173.78

That's a total savings of $20,465.69 for those of you keeping score!

Another alternative is to take classes online. Some schools even offer entire degrees online. There is a stereotype that online degrees aren't "real" degrees or they aren't as difficult as traditional ones, but that sentiment is slowly changing as more and more big schools offer online only instruction. The option is great for those of you who'd prefer not to leave the comfort of your room, but you have to have more self-discipline here because there's more opportunity to procrastinate. If you don't have to be online at certain times of day, you might have a tendency to put if off until you have half a semester's worth of classes to take before your midterm. Know yourself. If you know you need structure, this path will be more difficult for you.

Check out these sites for more information about online degrees.

http://www.geteducated.com

http://oedb.org

http://www.worldwidelearn.com/

Delay Going to College

Another option is to delay going to college. Enter the workforce first, save up the money, and then apply. Few students appear to exercise this option. Bozick and DeLuca reference the National Educational Longitudinal Study of 1988 in their academic paper *Better Late Than Never? Delayed Enrollment in the High School to College Transition*. The paper states: "16 percent of high school graduates postpone enrollment by seven months or more after completing high school." The authors go on to say that the common characteristic among these students are low socioeconomic resources or poor grades.

In talking with current high school students and old classmates, I tried to better understand the stigma around not going to college right away.

Certainly there is a social aspect to it. So many of our friends go to college right away, and the vast majority of students at Universities are between 18 and 22. It almost feels as if you're getting left behind if you don't go, but is delaying college really all that bad?

Social stature aside, let's say you enter the workforce right away and start making $30,000 a year. If you get your own place, you'll most likely need roommates to afford it. Let's take the following monthly budget as a starting point:

Income after taxes	$2,000
Rent	$450
Groceries	$320
Fast Food	$100
Utilities	$120
Misc	$100
Health Insurance (high deductible)	$80
Gas	$300
Car Payment	$160
Car Insurance	$110
Cell Phone	$60
Money left for savings	$200

Let's say you work 4 years and get a 3% raise each year. Keeping expenses the same, you'd save about: $14,000.

Now you can take that money and subtract it from either of the two plans we looked at above.

4-year University

Principal owed	$36,367
Annual rate	4.5%
Repayment period	10 years
Number of payments	120
Monthly payments	$376.90
Total paid over life of the loan	$45,228.22

2-years Community College, 2-years University

Principal owed	$19,911
Annual rate	4.5%
Repayment period	10 years
Number of payments	120
Monthly payments	$206.35
Total paid over life of the loan	$24,762.53

With either approach, you pay $17,411.25 less in student loans, and you have much more manageable monthly repayment options.

Make Your Opportunities

Whatever your choice, you need to make the decision for you. Ignore expectations and external pressures; if you truly want to succeed in college…in anything, the decision must come from you.

If you do decide that college is right for you, you'll be faced with a lot of new opportunities and challenges. College is a time to acquire as much knowledge as possible. You will be hard pressed to find any other place where there is a collection of people dedicated to helping you realize your own goals. Finishing college doesn't grant you any special privileges or rights. It's what you do with your time at college that will shape your first few years in the workforce.

College is an incredible experience if you make it one. You'll have so many chances to try new things, and you'll probably wind up doing something you never dreamed of. You'll meet people from all walks of life, make new friends, and experience a little bit more freedom and responsibility. You might join a club, a sports team, or maybe you'll study abroad. Whatever you choose to do, college is the place to expand your horizons and truly make something of yourself.

Now before we get ahead of ourselves, let's bring things back to the present. You still have a ton of questions I'm sure. Right now, your mind is probably cluttered with thoughts about the SAT, classes, schoolwork, application deadlines, scholarship essays, and whatever else you've got going on. Sometimes it's hard enough just to stay sane, much less enjoy your senior year. Everyone tells you to hang on to those moments because you'll miss them when they're gone, but if you're like I was, you can't wait to get out of high school. High school was great, sure, but you've got your eyes on something more; otherwise, why read this book?

Next, we'll look at ways of narrowing down your college search. Fair warning: you'll have to do a little bit of soul searching.

Chapter 2

Finding the College with the Right Fit

Selecting a college is a big decision. Do you stay close to home or go out of state? Do you choose a big school or a small one? Did your family go to a certain school? Will you like the campus? What will you major in?

Whether you've had your dream school picked out your whole life or have no idea whatsoever, you should take the time to understand your chosen college. One size does not fit all, and just because many of your friends or older siblings go to one college, doesn't mean it's the right choice for you. Take some time. Consider your options.

One consistent truth in talking to different Universities is that it's really all about fit. Will you be a good fit at your school? That seems to be the biggest consideration on the minds of the admissions staff. This isn't to say that students who want to major in Liberal Arts won't get into an engineering-centric school, but each college has its own culture and values. Everything about a University from its motto and mentality to its staff and course offerings drive from the school's Charter. Spend some time to look around some school websites and see what their values are.

Do they align with yours?

Questions to Ask Yourself

Do you know what you want to study?

Most colleges offer a variety of majors, but many are known as technical schools, liberal arts schools, science schools, and so on. You'll want to choose a place where you won't be limited in your field. College is the time to enrich yourself, discover yourself, and challenge yourself. Vigorously pursue your passions in an environment where you have the most opportunity.

You don't have to know your specific major to have a general idea of what interests you. If you love crunching numbers, find out about good engineering schools. If you find you've more of a poet's soul, explore schools with great theater, writing, and art programs.

US News offers college rankings in different areas, but make sure you check the ranking criteria. Some of the scoring can be a little interesting. Search the Web for ideas, and don't judge a college by name or reputation. The truth is that you may get the best education at a University you've never heard of or even considered.

What do you want to be near?

The exciting metropolis of Manhattan is a far cry from the serene mountains in Boulder, CO. The warm and sunny beaches at Manoa are nothing like the crisp and rustic Amherst.

Where do you enjoy yourself?

You might be a hip urbanite, needing to keep your finger on the pulse of a busy city, or a soul searcher looking for a quieter scene. Maybe you'd rather hit the slopes every weekend or catch a wave before class. Look at life off-campus when you are choosing colleges.

Does your personality match your school's?

Perhaps you love getting caught up in the moment with a crowd of tens of thousands of other screaming football fans. You can unite behind a cause and feel like a part of something greater than yourself. You may consider looking into bigger schools. They often have lots of programs and clubs you can join.

On the other hand, maybe you're more of a self-starter. You'd rather form a club with like-minded individuals. Division I sports aren't that important to you. You spend your time standing out rather than being part of the crowd. A smaller school could be just the right fit for you.

Are you constantly plugged in? You might enjoy being in a high tech school. You would thrive in an innovative digital environment with the latest in advanced technology. Look into the school's living spaces, library, and classrooms. You may decide a newer school is the way to go.

Are you a history buff? You love old brick buildings and are absolutely fascinated by local history. You want to have a sense of tradition and would feel more at home in an older school.

These points are by no means definitive, nor are they meant to exclude different types of schools; they are simply meant to get you thinking about yourself and where you would fit best. Take a little time for introspection when you're choosing your future alma mater.

Do not choose a school because:

Your friends are going there

Your friends aren't you, and they shouldn't influence your decision. College is about exploring and meeting new people. Don't make the mistake of bringing high school drama with you to college.

This isn't to say you should go to a school where you don't know anyone either. Simply make the choice for yourself, and not because of someone else. Nobody can tell you where you belong.

If you get into the college of your choice and find that you're truly unhappy there, you can always arrange to transfer schools. Most schools require general education credits, so no matter what you take, it will likely transfer. Keep in mind that each school sets it own requirements for graduation and majors, so if you wait too long and work hard toward a degree at one school, transferring to another may mean taking a few more courses. This could push back your graduation date. There's no shame in graduating late, but it is an extra year's worth of tuition, books, and living expenses.

It is less expensive

Easier said than done, right? As you strike out on your own, money will most likely be a concern. This is where hunting for scholarships becomes a necessity. There's nothing like free money, but we'll get to that in another chapter. You don't want to look back and regret your choice just because it was cheaper for you to go there.

You have only one reason

What I mean by this is that if you want to go to school to play a sport, you're now at that school if things don't work out. College sports aren't like high school Varsity. Because they know you aren't in class constantly, coaches will present you with off-season schedules, and a lot of times it'll involve early morning runs, mid-day lifts, and evening drills. The sport will become your life, and you will become the property of your coach and the team. Not only that, but you represent your school, and you may have to dress appropriately. Some coaches don't allow their athletes to wear open-toed shoes.

If you're willing to make the commitment, and as anyone in the NCAA can tell you, plenty of students are, then go for it. Don't let anything hold you back and chase after your goal with as much gusto as you can muster. If you have doubts, don't worry, it's natural to have doubts, but ask yourself this question: if I end up quitting the team, will I still enjoy the school? If the answer is yes, no worries. But if you don't think you will, and you're not sure you want to play Varsity, then you've got some soul searching to do.

I would like to say, however, that though this is an important decision—it is not the most important of your life. As I mentioned before, you can transfer, and tens of thousands of students do each year. One of my best friends in college transferred from another school.

You're going to learn so much about yourself in the next coming years, so don't be surprised if you end up making different decisions down the road. It's called growth, and it's an inevitable side effect of exposing yourself to bigger and better things. Remember that college is about you and nobody else. It's not about where your friends are going, and it's not about the pressure you're under to get into a good school.

College is an institution of higher learning. You're meant to grow, cultivate your passions, explore your interests, and take advantage of the amazing opportunity ahead of you. It's not always easy to find an environment where making mistakes is ok and expected. At no other point will you be surrounded by intelligent people whose purpose is to help you achieve what it is you set out to do. You won't have the same access to professors, labs, computer technology, and information after college. Take full advantage of the incredible journey before you.

So you have the questions figured out, but how do you go about getting the information you need?

Finding Out More About A School

Online Research

Start with the website. Most schools have an FAQ section for prospective students, as well as a way to contact the school for further questions. Read their mission statement. Do you agree with it? Does it fit you?

Reach out to current students and recent alumni. School sites sometimes have a student blog section to talk about life on campus or in the area. Facebook is another great tool. See if there are any interest groups associated with the college. Don't necessarily go around friending random strangers, but reach out to people and see what they think. You might get some great advice.

Twitter is another great tool. Many college admissions offices are on Twitter now, and you can follow them to get updates about upcoming events and information.

Chances are you already know a few people that attend the school. Connect with them, even if you didn't know them that well. Most people are happy to give you their opinions.

And when you learn about the school, consider the source. Don't make a major decision based on what a friend heard. Rumors fly at light speed, and the only people best qualified to tell you about a college are the people involved with it. Make the effort to find out for yourself what a college is all about, and don't rely solely on opinion.

If you want more information, check out these great sites:

http://mycollegeguide.org/guru

http://collegeconfidential.com

http://nextstepu.com

http://allaboutcollege.com

http://knowhow2go.com

The Internet allows you to connect with people and information, but there's a lot of nonsense out there, too. You have to be mindful of what you read.

Picking a school is overwhelming at times, unless of course you've known for years you're destined for Vassar. For the rest of us though, there's a lot to consider, and it all centers around you and your personality. If nothing you've looked at so far has gotten you excited; if you've spent hours contemplating your dream school and just cannot come up with an idea, you can try an online personality quiz that matches you to a school.

There are several sites that offer to narrow down your college search. All you do is enter information about your desired degree and major; however, take the results with a grain of salt:

The less information you give, the less accurate the match is. How can you possibly expect a simple Website to understand your complex human nature based on a few text fields on a form?

These searches are based on computer algorithms that pigeonhole your answers to match one of several schools. There is no possible way for that search to understand your complexities, likes and interests, and therefore, your best choice of school.

Less scrupulous sites will serve up schools that pay to show up first. So rather than giving you an honest answer, they tell you what someone else is trying to sell you.

That being said, you might consider checking out a couple of different sites that do this to see if you get fairly consistent answers. One result isn't enough to make a judgment, but several similar results will give you a more accurate picture. Consider checking out:

http://collegegrazing.com

http://collegetrends.org

http://princetonreview.com/colleges-majors.aspx

Even though these sites are legitimate, their results are still based on a computer algorithm, and even if the site is the "Deep Thought" of college matching, no computer will ever be able to understand the peculiar needs of a person 100% of the time. Use these tools as a guide to get going in the right direction.

Honestly, there is no easy way to figure out what school you want to go to. You have to do the legwork and look into it. Don't trust anyone else to tell you who you are and where you belong. Take advice, sure. Look into recommendations, and research suggestions, but don't blindly accept what others tell you. They view life through their own lens of experience, and you yours. Being unique means you aren't exactly like anyone else, so ultimately, you have to decide what is right for you.

College Fairs and Campus Visits

Go to college fairs and get exposed to schools you may not have even heard of. Who knows? You may stumble upon your perfect school. These fairs usually require a bit of travel, but so do campus visits. There may be a college fair in your school, but if all else fails, try nacacnet.org to find the National Association of College Admissions Counselors list of fairs.

After you're comfortable that you found some great choices, make a short list of schools. You should target four or five, and make plans to visit each campus. Technology is amazing but a virtual tour will never compare to going in person. You can take that opportunity to talk to current students and get their opinions of the school. Often times, the school will have "ambassadors" that are more than happy to tell you about their experiences.

Make sure to visit during the semester and during a weekday if possible. You'll want to see the school the way it is normally, and if everyone's on vacation, you'll wind up seeing a lot of nice buildings and not many people. Some schools are heavy commuter schools, meaning most of the students live off campus, and so they're not there on the weekend. Go when there are students around, and ask them about campus life. Find out what things are like during the week versus the weekend. Talk to freshmen because they're the most like you at this point, still new to the scene and adjusting. They'll give you a good idea of what you're first few weeks will be like. Also, talk to upperclassmen as well; they've been around longer and have more experience going to that school.

Here are a few questions you can ask:

What's been the biggest change for you since coming to college?

Is there a lot to do outside of class?

Do most events happen on or off campus?

What types of events happen on campus?

What is transportation like? Do most students drive? Does the University provide buses? If so, do they go into town? Are the buses free or do you have to pay?

Keep in mind that not every student is going to be satisfied with the school. Disregard anyone that tells you the school sucks and gives you flimsy reasons. If, however, most of the students you talk to say the same negative things, you can pretty much take that at face value. Try to find students involved in organizations you'd like to join. They'll most likely try to recruit you, but they clearly enjoy the school if they're encouraging you to go there.

When you visit, make sure to get a guided tour. Often times, larger schools offer tours only on certain days, and the group sizes are limited, so check the website or call in to see what the policies are and when the next tours are.

You'll want to take the time to wander around campus with just your family. First of all, it's good to have some extra pairs of eyes with you to take everything in. Imagine a typical day. Start at the dorms and see what the commute to the academic buildings is like. Can you see yourself doing that several times a week?

Make sure to visit the library. University libraries are some of the best and most comprehensive around. They are invaluable centers for research and study, and you'll need to do a lot of both over the next few years.

If you have an idea of what you want to study, it wouldn't hurt to look and see what their collection is like. Ask how easy it is to obtain a book that's not in the library. Can they order it for you? How long would that usually take?

Furthermore, check out their computer labs. Technology being the way it is, you need to stay up to date regardless of your field, and especially so if you want to major in Information Systems or a tech-related field.

Visit the admissions office and sit down with an advisor. You have to make appointments for these, so plan your day around it. Prepare a list of questions, and print them out before you go: don't expect yourself to remember every question you had. Talk with your parents, and see what their concerns are. Be sure to bring them up with the admissions advisor. Here are a few questions to get you started:

What percentage of the students live off campus?

What dining options are there?

Is there a health clinic on campus? (For potential injuries)

Does the school offer health insurance for its students?

What is the average cost of living on campus? Off campus?

Is the campus safe or protected? Are there police officers onsite? If not, do they respond quickly?

Have there ever been any violent incidents on campus?

Does your school have an organization that [your interest]?

How easy is it for students to start an organization?

Where is the financial aid office?

What percentage of students get job offers before and immediately after graduating? If you know your major, this would be a better question for the head of that department since it varies. I can tell you, engineers get jobs much more quickly than English majors.

Once you've finished up with admissions, pay a visit to the financial aid office. They'll not only tell you what's available, they'll even give you the applications and next steps to take. Take a folder with you to carry everything, and don't lose it. If you're visiting multiple colleges on your trip, take one folder for each campus because you don't want to get the forms for different Universities mixed up.

Once you've spent a good amount of time around campus, take a drive around the nearby town. Get a feel for the area early on. Plan a meal with your family, and ask them what they think of the school. It's a good way to unwind and gather your thoughts after a long day.

Above all, don't get mired down in details. This is supposed to be a great time in your life, so enjoy it as best you can. College is exciting; it's okay to have fun.

Remember that college isn't as much about prestige as it is fit. In your application, you have to show where you fit the school, but you ultimately have the upper hand because you get to choose the school that fits you, and with more than 4,000 colleges in the United States alone, there is one out there that is perfect for you. You'll make some lifelong friends, and you won't be able to relive this time years down the road, so make the best of it now.

Chapter 3

Interviews with Universities

I spent several months corresponding and interviewing a variety of well-known Universities from across the country. My goal was to get a good cross-section of schools, small and large, urban and rural. Some are well known for their athletic programs, while others are known more for their alternative cultural lifestyles.

These questions came from a poll I conducted of several high school students. Many of their questions boiled down to the same ones. I picked from the most popular and the most interesting. These are real questions from real high school students.

Over the next several pages, you'll find out whether or not you really should do an extra-curricular activity; you'll find out what to include in your admissions essay, and you'll learn several things that colleges hate to see in an application.

I've quoted each response either as it was sent to me or transcribed from a phone interview. I wanted to illustrate the variety of answers I got. If you'd like to see all of the answers from a specific college, you can find them in the Appendix at the end of this book. Responses are in no particular order.

Can a person who has little to no extra-curricular activities expect a good chance of being accepted?

> *Florida State University* - While it is possible to be accepted to Florida State University with little or no extracurricular activities, the typical student that we admit is both academically strong and socially engaged.

> *University of Colorado: Boulder* - I think they do have a very good chance of being accepted. Part of the reason is that Admissions Counselors and professionals need to be very careful for making judgments they're not sure of. If somebody doesn't have a lot of ECs, we could make a judgment that they aren't involved, but we don't know the family dynamic. The student may have a significant responsibility in the home. Maybe they have to help raise family members; they have a job, or maybe they have an illness that precludes them from participating. I know many top academic students that do well in class but are light on the ECs. I'd love to have those students at the University of Colorado.

> One of the things we talk about at UC, we want to look for a good student and a good citizen. What I mean by that is not only being involved in the high school or community, but also to

make it a better place or are doing meaningful things in their life outside of the classroom, whether through organized activities or not.

University of Maryland: Baltimore County - It depends on the institution. There are a couple of scenarios to take into consideration: Student A, who has no extra-curricular activity but does well academically and student B who has a myriad of extra-curricular activities and average grades. For student A, imagine if every student who applied to "blank" university had a 4.5 weighted GPA and a 2400 SAT? The question to ask is what distinguishes this student from the other applicants? Also take into consideration for student A limited availability of seats for the incoming freshman class. If student A applied to an institution where limited enrollment does not exist, then student A would be a prime candidate. For student B, generally speaking, extra-curricular activities are looked upon favorably; however, extra-curricular activities do not replace sub-par grades.

So here we have three different answers from three different schools. A large school like Florida State implies that you need to be socially engaged outside of school to be competitive in their admissions process. UC Boulder on the other hand, has a completely different take, which speaks to their differing attitudes. UMBC points out that all else being equal, extra-curricular activities help a student to stand out.

One aside I'd like to mention here is that if you do decide to do things outside of school, don't do them just to bolster your college application. It actually hurts you to be too involved because you can't possibly contribute or learn anything meaningful if you're rushing from activity to activity. Pick one or two things that genuinely interest you and dedicate yourself to them. Be selective with your time.

Does it look better to take both the ACT and SAT, or does it matter?

Florida State University - We recommend that applicants take both exams since we use the best composite/total score for admission purposes.

Virginia Tech - It really does not matter which, or how many, tests are taken (though we absolutely do *not* advise taking standardized tests too many times -- in other words, we would advise against a number of test sittings that are excessive for the student's finances and/or performance). We in no way penalize students for the number or type of tests taken and take care to use only the highest score of any section from any test. We do not have a preference for the ACT or SAT – either or both is fine. (If they do take both, we will consider all scores reported. In other words, we would take the highest Critical Reading from the SAT and the highest math from the ACT for use in an applicant's review, if those were the highest scores for the applicant in question.)

University of Colorado: Boulder - We are very clear that we don't have a preference. We take either, but if we were to provide advice, we recommend they take both because they are different tests. One test may fit a student's style better and she may be more comfortable with it. We leave that to the student since there is no preference. We consider the highest score.

The other thing that college admissions officers are doing when they are reviewing an application is looking for a reason to admit rather than a reason to deny, so we want to give a student credit for the higher score.

The University of Hawai'i at Mānoa - has no preference to either test, we will accept both. However, for the ACT, students must take the writing category to be considered.

Also, if the student takes the test multiple times (either the SAT or ACT), we will take the highest score in each category. For example, if a student scores a 500/510/530 on the SAT the first time and a 520/540/510 the second time, we will report scores as 520/540/530.

In this case, there seems to be a little more agreement between colleges. You're free to take either, and it may make sense for you to take both, but don't overdo it in retakes.

What do you look for in a good admissions essay? Is it more important to be grammatically correct or engaging?

University of North Carolina - We like to see that a student understands the rules of grammar. We do hope that they take some time to proofread or ask someone else to look it over. We love to see an engaging essay where the content is captivating. Each year, applicants continue to amaze us. It is incredible to see how far a student will take an admissions essay whether it's about their academic interests or humor. We always love seeing humor.

University of Maryland: Baltimore County - In a college admissions essay, it is important for the student to stay on topic and present a grammatically sound essay. Essentially, the essay gives prospective students the opportunity to demonstrate academic talent beyond a GPA and test score. Different institutions place different weighting on the essay. For some institutions, the essay accounts for 30 percent of the admissions review process and in others it may only account for 5 percent. To add another layer to the essay, aside from general admissions, some schools offer honors and scholars programs along with select scholarship opportunities. For these opportunities, the essay can become increasingly significant as certain courses in the above programs may be writing intensive and the committee members are looking for a success predictor.

Oklahoma State University - OSU's admission and scholarship questions from the application for admission are used to award certain scholarships as well as help determine holistic and alternative admission candidates.

These questions allow applicants to highlight their involvement in school, work, community service, and other organizations. It is important applicants demonstrate their best possible writing ability both in content and grammar, however, community involvement and demonstrated and potential leadership skills are also evaluated.

The Universities I spoke with consistently point out that essays should have interesting, polished content. Because there's so much latitude in the essay, it's good to know the personality and culture of your school; for example, UNC specifically mentions liking to see humor.

How big of a role do recommendation letters play in the application? Is there anything you would tell a student about whom to ask to recommend him/her?

Duke University - We look for insight from letters of recommendation, particularly with respect to the kind of student someone is. I tell students that they should get letters of recommendations from the teachers for whom they've done their best work.

University of Colorado: Boulder - Pick the faculty member that can really speak to your ability to succeed in college. We've seen students pick the most difficult subjects and the teachers that go with that, with the idea that if they pick the toughest subject it will be more impressive. That person may not be able to write as well about the student than another faculty member that has known that student for a long time. Sometimes students make that mistake of analyzing who they want to write their letters for them and picking the appropriate individual.

The other mistake students will sometimes make is not giving their teachers enough time to write a good letter. Students should always give their faculty members ample time. The faculty member has a lot of priorities, and if you give her only two days to write a letter for you, she shouldn't give you much effort. If you give her a few weeks, a copy of your resume, and other achievements, so she is prepared and has enough time to write you a really good letter.

University of North Carolina - We require a teacher recommendation and a counselor statement. It's important to think carefully and select a teacher that has known them for some time and has a clear understanding of their academic potential. A teacher from a core academic area from English to Math would be best, but most importantly choose a teacher that knows you well.

The University of Hawai'i at Mānoa - Although letters of recommendation are not required, they can help strengthen an application. They do not guarantee admission for students but can definitely help us better understand the applicant. Letters of recommendation can be most beneficial to a student if there is an area in which they are lacking. For example, if a student scores low on the math portion of the SAT but performs better in the classroom, a letter from a math teacher that can highlight the student's ability can help.

Oklahoma State University - Oklahoma State University encourages applicants to submit letters of recommendation, specifically to address areas in which there may be remediations. Recommendation letters should be written by representatives that the applicant has known for at least a year and that can address academic areas of concern. Letters of recommendation are used most often by the Admission Review Committee that evaluates students for holistic and alternative admission.

Whether or not you have to submit letters of recommendation, it's good to have a few on hand. They can only strengthen the application.

How far does knowing a foreign language go in getting accepted to a University?

Florida State University - Two sequential units of the same foreign language are required for admission to Florida State; however, we prefer students to challenge themselves by taking additional years of the same foreign language.

University of Maryland: Baltimore County - For most institutions, a foreign language is not "required" to gain admission into the university. Keep in mind if the student is applying to a liberal arts institution, there is a language requirement to graduate from the university. In that vein, it is beneficial to the student to have high school foreign language experience so that he/she may be able to test out or test into a higher level language class to complete the language requirement sooner. On the other hand, if a student is applying directly to a foreign affairs program at "blank" institution, having language proficiency may be mandatory for admission. It is also important to address students with documented learning disabilities. If the student has an IEP in high school that exempted the student from taking a foreign language, an exception can be made at the post-secondary level.

Virginia Tech - Because we do not require a foreign language as part of the admissions criteria, not having a foreign language will not necessarily hurt a strong applicant's chances; however, we certainly favorably view applicants who have taken strong academic courses that will help them prepare for college, and a sequence of foreign language would look more favorable than several non-academic electives on a transcript. We also recommend that students take advantage of the courses (if available) while in high school since foreign language is a required subject for graduation from Virginia Tech and can be fulfilled by gaining sufficient credit while still in high school (which could potentially free their schedule up for other courses at Virginia

Tech, if they are admitted).

For the most part, schools look at foreign language credit favorably. Some schools require them while others don't. Colleges usually take availability of courses into consideration as well. If you didn't have a lot of opportunity to learn another language, it wouldn't count against you. Generally, schools that say their mission is to prepare their students for a "global world" will more likely look for foreign language credits than others that don't, which ties back into the school's culture.

Are there any pet peeves you have when seeing poor applications?

Florida State University - A sloppy application is my biggest pet peeve. If the student does not care, why should I? In addition, we correspond to our students by email. I would recommend students having a separate email account for the application process. Some of the email addresses are just not appropriate for the application process.

Virginia Tech - Students who do not follow instructions (miss deadlines, fail to check the online status page we provide them to be sure their transcripts and scores are received, etc.) and then ask for special treatment as a result take up a lot of our time. Misspelling words that high school seniors should know, and generally not showing that care was taken with their application materials are other problems we see often.

University of Colorado: Boulder - No and yes. I think the thing that is sometimes concerning is when a University is asking a set of very important questions about who a student is. In our essay, we talk about the importance of diversity in higher education. There are so many kinds of diversity, not just racial, but geographic and academic. If you are going to join a community that values diversity, it looks bad when you spend little or no time addressing that. It's disconcerting because that's somebody we're looking to make part of our student body.

When the application is put together very quickly or without much thought, admissions officers would find that a concern. If students are interested in joining our campus community, we want to know the questions are worth their time and effort. It's rushing and hurrying through this process that's the biggest concern.

Fortunately now that applications are online, problems such as illegibility, stains etc are disappearing.

Another thing we want students to do is for them to realize it's a business relationship with the college, not a social one. You have to make sure your communication style is professional. The application is a time to be more formal.

We get email addresses that are very revealing. There are email addresses that can be used in the social environment with your friends, but when we don't know the applicant, we prefer to see a more professional email address. You're submitting documents to an individual you may not have met, so it's best to put your best foot forward.

University of Maryland: Baltimore County - Pet Peeves, no as the admissions process has to remain objective and fair. However, I would like to stress the importance of putting accurate information on the application. For example, if the student does not know his/her social security number, he/she should double check before submitting the application. An incorrect social security number prevents admissions staff from matching appropriate documents with the student. This in turn can slow down the application review process.

University of North Carolina - Rather than focus on what we don't like to see, we prefer applications where students have taken the time to provide as much information as possible about themselves. We can tell if a student has waited until the last minute in terms of carelessness in spelling and grammar. We like to see applications that are thoughtfully prepared and really demonstrate an interest in Carolina.

The University of Hawai'i at Mānoa - Personally, some of my pet peeves are illegible hand writing, unprofessional e-mail addresses (i.e. ilovevideogames@hotmail.com versus having their first and last name), and essays that have not been proof-read and are not personalized to the school (i.e. writing, "Dear Princeton" when it is being sent to University of Hawai'i at Mānoa). I should note however, that although these are "pet peeves" they do not affect a student's admissibility to the University.

Duke University - Lack of effort in filling out the application. That's really the only thing that rubs me the wrong way.

This question got the most intriguing answers, which is why I included so many responses. Each one is different and really reflects the personality of each school and each admissions officer. It pays to be aware of what not to do.

Are previously rejected applications given equal consideration for the next term?

Florida State University - We will reconsider all applicants who apply for another term. I would hope they would submit additional documentation.

University of Colorado: Boulder - We don't automatically reconsider applications, but each new submitted application is considered fresh. A lot of times we try to work with a student to outline steps for him to gain admission to the University. To students who are reapplying, we think that is outstanding, and we certainly want to help them, and a lot of times there is new academic material in the application.

University of Maryland: Baltimore County - The term equal consideration can be a little misleading. If the student applies and is not offered admission and the student does nothing differently, then, the student will not be offered admission for the next term. However, some institutions allow for the student to submit additional test scores or a final transcript (with a strong upward trend) for additional review. Sometimes, all the student has to do is demonstrate academic success at a post-secondary institution for one semester and resubmit their interest in the original institution and can receive a favorable result.

University of North Carolina - If we aren't able to offer admissions, they won't be able to be accepted for a following cycle; however transfer applications are considered differently, in that we don't see if they applied before. Each application is a new start. Transfer admission is a lot less competitive because there are far fewer applications for each slot. We receive nearly 3000 transfer student applications for 800 slots rather than 24,000 new student applications for 4000 slots.

What is the most important character trait an applicant should have?

Virginia Tech - An applicant (who may possibly be a student in the future at our respective school) should be **respectful**!

Duke University - The most important character trait is integrity;

without that nothing else matters. But assuming the integrity is there, we look for strong academic and intellectual ability, the inclination to take advantage of opportunities, and the willingness to be a contributing member of a diverse and interesting community of talented individuals. Students with these characteristics, who reveal in their applications that they will offer something valuable to the community and benefit from being part of that community often find themselves with lots of good choices when it comes to the college admissions process. It's difficult to describe exactly how one student distinguishes himself or herself in a pool of almost 30,000 applicants.

Oklahoma State University - There is rarely one particular trait an applicant should have, however we encourage students to showcase their academic, as well as leadership abilities and potential. By revealing more than scholarly abilities, a student can showcase other interests, which may lead to scholarly pursuits, study abroad, campus life or research interests during his or her academic career.

Florida State University - We would hope all of our applicants would be honest, well-round individuals who embrace leadership, learning, service, and global awareness. In fact our essay question on the application addresses this – "Florida State University is more than just a world-class academic institution preparing you for a future career. We are a caring community of well-rounded individuals who embrace leadership, learning, service, and global awareness. With this in mind, which of these characteristics appeal most to you, and why?"

University of Colorado: Boulder - I can't single out the most important, but here are several: honor, integrity, appreciating similarities and differences between people, and someone who is academically engaged, are four traits we are continually looking for. We are also looking for someone who gives back to their community. We want to see someone who knows the world is bigger than their sphere.

If it came down to one trait, it would be academic preparedness. We don't want students to come here for a semester or a year and leave, we want them to come here and graduate. So the ability to assess academic preparedness in the classroom would probably lead the way.

University of Maryland: Baltimore County - In general, the strongest trait a student should have is the gift of decision making. Rather than apply to 30 schools, students should thoroughly research 3 or 4 schools then the student will make the best use of his/her time and energy. Regarding the actual applicant, I would recommend that the student make a plan in high school to be the best he or she can be without excuses. As admissions professionals, we do not know the student personally so the student truly has to "look good on paper." While there are extenuating circumstances, "Sara just does not test well," is not a solid excuse to reverse an admission decision.

University of North Carolina - It's hard to identify just one. We look for kindness and compassion, overall integrity. We don't value one over the other. Students amaze and surprise us with what they bring to the table. We like to see diverse experiences and a diverse outlook on life. It's hard to pin it down to one trait.

The University of Hawai'i at Mānoa - Self-initiative. Students who take control of their own application show the student's maturity and desire to attend the University and something THEY want and not an influence of anyone else (parents, teachers, friends, etc).

What captured my attention most during these interviews is how differently each University answered this question. There are certainly some common themes, like honesty and integrity. We also see decisiveness, respectfulness, and preparedness as some other highly sought-after traits.

Is there any general advice you have for college applicants?

The University of Hawai'i at Mānoa - My advice to students is to take every opportunity to learn something about college and the schools that they are interested in. Attend college fairs, high school visits, take a campus tour and attend special events sponsored by the University. If possible, do this early. The more experience the student has, the better they can make a decision on where they want to go and what will be the right fit.

I also highly encourage asking questions, no matter how big or small. College is an opportunity to change and create a new and exciting future for one self. If a student does not ask questions, they will not get the answers and will not learn, and learning is what college is all about!

Florida State University - Preparation for the college application process does not begin in the senior year. It starts as early as middle school when selecting challenging courses and progressing through high school with a rigorous course schedule. There is no need to apply to 10-15 colleges. Do your research to determine what you really want in your future college and apply to schools that are a good fit. As all colleges will emphasize, "It's a match to be made, not a prize to be won." And finally celebrate all the acceptances with your family, and don't take the "no's" personally.

Virginia Tech - Applicants should take care to note specific requirements (and due dates) for all of the various schools to which they are applying, as they can vary widely. We consider it the applicant's responsibility to keep up with each school's requirements, not the other way around. We assume that a student who is truly interested in attending our university will take the time and make an effort to follow our clear instructions.

Oklahoma State University - Work with your admissions counselor! We are here to help and look forward to working with prospective students and families throughout the process.

University of Colorado: Boulder - The only advice I would give is to find a way to manage the time that the application process takes. I'm not just referring to the admission application. Students are so busy, then they hit their final year, they have all these applications and financial aid and scholarships. Then they have to fill out housing applications and orientation forms. It can be a lot of hurried paperwork if you don't manage your time.

Get an early start, and keep on top of the deadlines; you can dial down the anxiety in the whole process.

Duke University - Students should love every college on their list. Don't apply to a school you don't want to attend. College admissions is full of so much uncertainty now, make sure that every college you're applying to is one you'd be happy to attend.

University of North Carolina - Don't wait until the last minute. We can tell when applications are thrown together. It's important to begin cultivating relationships with teachers now so you can get a great recommendation later. Don't wait until the last minute until the essay. We generally post essay questions in the summer, so you can start now and begin practicing. Essay questions are published on our Website.

So now you've got the gist that each school is different in its expectations and requirements. The important thing to take away is that yes, you need to prepare your application well ahead of time if you're going to stand a decent chance of making it in. Not to worry though, the next chapter will walk you through typical application sections and show you how to get them done quickly and efficiently.

Chapter 4

How to Crush Your Application

By this point, you should have done some preliminary research and narrowed down your short list to 5 or 6 schools. I'd even advise narrowing the list down to 3: your reach school, a close second, and a safety. You don't want to spend too much money on application fees with a shotgun approach. Plus, it will help you focus on your applications for those you do choose.

In this chapter, I'm going to show you how to put together a stellar application. We'll go over the different sections using the Common Application as a guide. Along the way, I'll provide you tips that will make you stand out and make the process feel easy.

Applications change from year to year, but they all have one purpose: to help admissions reviewers decide if you're a good fit for the school. They aren't looking for reasons to disqualify you.

First, I think it's helpful to put the Application into perspective. In many ways it's a lot like a resume. Both are limited in what they say about you, so you have to make sure that what they do say represents the best of what you have to offer. Imagine you're shooting a commercial about you. You've got your audience's attention for a brief time in between many other commercials. You have to stand out from the white noise somehow and catch your viewer's attention.

Your application has to reflect who you are, what you want, and why you should get in. You have to take your time and put in the effort because a lazy application won't get you in anywhere. I know it's tough. Between all of the other things you have going on—classes, SATs, and other activities—you've got to work on college applications.

I have one word for you: prioritize. Don't fly through the application just to get it done and get back to your life. Sloppy commercials don't sell, and neither do sloppy applications. Start working now so you aren't overwhelmed when deadlines approach.

When to Apply

You'll want to do early application if possible, which is usually the winter before you want to attend, but check with the college Website to make sure. Applying early offers loads of benefits including hearing back sooner about the admissions decision, and more time to look for scholarships and apply for housing.

So you'll want to start thinking about colleges your junior year. Take the SAT or ACT, and get it out of the way. Senior year will be hectic enough.

Stressing out over these tests is not something you want on your shoulders as a senior. Of course, if you're going to retake them to get higher scores, at least you have that option and have already had exposure to the test.

Being selective about the schools you apply to will also help cut out the stress. That's why I recommend around 3. On the flip side, you might think applying to one would be even more focused. I'm all for the power of positive thinking, but that's too much risk to take on.

Applying to more than one school is by no means an expectation of failure – it's a fail-safe. Every semester, any college deals with thousands upon thousands of applications, but there is only so much space on campus, so many buildings, and so many classrooms, with only so many seats. Universities cannot accommodate every qualified applicant.

A number of things can happen during the application process; for instance, your school may never have forwarded your transcripts, you may have forgotten to send your SAT scores, or you sent a good, complete application, but there were an unusual number of highly-qualified early applicants that semester.

Imagine you apply to your top school and none other – but you only find out (well after the deadline) that you forgot something vital in your application packet. You don't have the time to apply to other schools, so you might as well enjoy your year at home and get a temp job.

So even if you know for certain what school you most want to attend, plan for some back-ups. It's better to have the security of a fallback than be left back.

When you have your list of schools, revisit their websites and put all of the key deadlines on a calendar. Work on the application early so that you won't miss anything, and you'll have the time to review your application before sending it in. This will force you to collect all the information you need sooner rather than later. Having that information so soon will come in handy because you'll need them for scholarships.

If on the other hand you're a procrastinator, and there are plenty of you out there, the National Association of College Admissions Counselors posts vacancies after the May 1 deadline at http://www.nacac.com. But if you wind up putting off your college applications until after the deadline, you've got some habits you need to fix right away.

A Look at the Application

Colleges want to have a diverse student body. This doesn't mean they have race/ethnic quotas or anything like that. In fact, I don't know of any that favor anyone on the basis of race. Colleges want a student body that will succeed. Successful alumni draw attention and good press to the school, in turn allowing them to get more high quality applicants and alumni donations. Colleges invest a lot of money in becoming better centers of learning. They offer countless opportunities for anyone willing to look for them. So when an applicant comes along that looks like an expert at making the best of their opportunities, they are naturally more appealing to admissions officers.

I'd like to make the point here that "making the best of your opportunities" does not mean signing up to every club, sport, and volunteer activity you possibly can. You can't do everything. The human brain is capable of working at a high-capacity level for so many hours in a day. After that, you'll suffer from mental fatigue. When you participate in several activities, you can only operate at full capacity for so long. After that, you're on autopilot. You go through the motions and cease to learn anything.

Imagine that you have to defend your choices to an admissions officer. Don't only think of what you can learn, but think of what you could contribute to any club you join. Students that show they can give back are much better suited to success.

Next, let's take a look at what you'll need to have. You can find the Common Application online at http://www.commonapp.org. I encourage you to sign up for a free account and follow along as we go. Over 400 universities use this same form, including Vassar, Yale, Vanderbilt, University of Pennsylvania, University of Massachusetts, and UCONN just to name a few. The nice thing about the Common App is that it helps you cut down on the time you spend filling out the same information across applications for different schools.

See any schools you like on the Common App site? If so, click around, and see if they require anything more than just the Application, like SAT subject tests or multiple essays. It's better to have a sense of the work ahead of you early.

Here are the major sections of the Common App (as of February 2015) along with some information you'll need to start gathering:

- Profile – typical stuff like name, gender, address, etc.

  o Personal Information

  o Address

  o Contact details (email and phone number)

  o Demographics

  o Geography

  o Language

  o Citizenship

  o Common App Fee Waiver

- Family – information about your parents and siblings

  o Household (parents marital status, etc)

  o Parent 1 (name, occupation, education level)

  o Parent 2 (name, occupation, education level)

  o Sibling (name, age, education level)

- Education

  o Current or Most Recent School

- Month and Year of entry

- Graduation Date

- Counselor's name, job title, email and phone number

o Other Schools

o Community-Based Organizations

- Organization Name

- Counselor's name, job title, email, and phone number

o Education Interruption (if you didn't or won't attend high school continuously)

o College and Universities (if you have taken college courses)

- College name

- Months and Years attended

- Degree Earned

o Grades

- Class rank

- Graduating class size

- Cumulative GPA

- GPA Scale

- GPA Weighting
  - Current Year Courses
    - How many courses
    - Course scheduling system used by the school
    - Course Title (for each course)
    - Level of Course (for each course)
  - Honors
    - Number of Honors received
    - Title of Honors
    - Grade level
    - Level of recognition
  - Future Plans
    - Career interest
    - Highest degree you intend to earn
- Testing
  - Tests you've taken
  - Grades received on each test (SAT, ACT, etc)
  - Number of future sittings you expect for each test
- Activities (max of 10)
  - Type

- o   Position/Leadership description

- o   Details/honors won/accomplishments

- o   Participation grade levels

- o   Timing of participation

- o   Hours spent per week

- o   Weeks spent per year

- o   Intent to continue the activity in college

- Personal Essay (250-650 words)

As you can see, there's a good amount of information. You might need to track down some names, phone numbers, and email addresses of your counselors from school and other activities.

The good news is, once this data prep is done, you've gotten it out of the way; however, you might also have to submit additional information if you're trying to get into a special program. For example, you might have to take an SAT subject test, or you might have to submit a portfolio of your work for an art school. Make sure you find out what all is required for the programs you want to apply to.

The Most Important Parts of Your Application

A lot of the information in the Application is pretty cut and dry. There's no ambiguity on what you need to put for your name and family. Still, there are ways you can be a little creative and stand out from the rest.

From my research, I've been able to boil down the most important parts of the application. These are the things you absolutely must have if you're hoping to get into your top choice school.

The High School Academic Transcript

The academic transcript is the single most important thing in the Application. Colleges want you to succeed: that's one of the major criteria they use to evaluate whether or not they should admit you. A poor GPA will significantly limit your options.

You're in school to learn. Your transcript is treated as an indicator of how well you learn, so a higher GPA should equate to traits such as preparedness, critical thinking, and diligence. Every successful student needs these traits.

I'm not saying that the other parts of the Application aren't important. They just aren't as strong of indicators as the transcript and here's why: the transcript tells what kind of student you are. It shows your grades and how challenging your course load was. An ideal transcript will have a mix of good grades and challenging courses. You don't have to be a straight-A, all-AP-classes type of student to succeed. Even if you are AP-level and your school doesn't offer them, that won't count against you. Admissions reviewers have to consider your background, circumstances, and opportunities you had available to you.

Realize that you must set the bar for yourself and not worry about what others are doing. So your best friend is a math person, and you aren't. It doesn't mean you need to keep up with him to appeal to colleges. Take what challenges you, not your friend. Some people are numbers people. Others are artistic. Some have great attention to detail, and others are great at seeing the big picture. There is room in the world for everyone. So bear this in mind when you're choosing your junior and senior classes: go after what challenges you, but be careful not to burn yourself out.

Hopefully you're reading this book early enough to make changes if you need to. Your strengths and weaknesses are different from everyone else's. Take the classes that push you outside your comfort zone because there are two things you don't want to do:

> Get great grades in easy courses. This might show that you're lazy and prefer the easy path rather than challenging yourself.

> Get terrible grades in very difficult courses. This could show that you're a poor judge of your capabilities or that you're not able to tell when you're in over your head.

If you know your GPA isn't up to where it should be, then work extra hard to bring it up. Consider dropping out of some extra-curricular activities if need be. I cannot stress enough how important it is to make the grades.

The good news is that even if you have a low GPA now, if you can bring it up and consistently show improvement, then that's a powerful story. Your cumulative may be on the low side, but if you can show you can consistently get good grades over your senior year, you still may impress the admissions board. You've shown that when you buckle down and get serious, you can succeed. That's what colleges want to see.

Test Scores (ACT or SAT)

These tests are meant to gauge your aptitude (ability to learn) and not what you already know. You don't need a 2200 to get into a college. If you've got a good GPA, colleges are willing to be more lenient on the test scores. Some students just can't take tests well. The SAT and ACT are taken on a particular day during a three hour period. You could be Einstein at 3 pm and Tweedle Dumb at 9 am, and those morning tests just don't bring out the best in you. That's why your GPA is given the most weight—it is the most convenient measurement of your abilities and work ethic over a period of time.

Test scores by themselves are not reliable indicators of success in college. They only really matter when compared to other parts of the application. For instance, a 590 verbal score from a student from a competitive school whose parents both went to college isn't that big of a deal. That same score from an inner city student whose parents didn't graduate high school is much more impressive.

If you need extra help with test taking, it's a good idea to seek help outside of class. Whether your school offers an SAT Prep course or you take one through a third party, like Kaplan, do whatever it takes to get the best grade possible. Don't make it hard to admit you. Make it easy.

Essay

A lot of students stress over the essay. But I'm here to tell you not to worry. The essay isn't meant for you to guess at what you think a college wants to see. It's also not meant to showcase your ability to use a thesaurus. You are a high school student, and the person that reviews your application will know that. Colleges don't expect you to churn out graduate-level stuff.

The essay should be good, honest writing. With it, you can demonstrate your attention to detail, your thought process, and your personality. With good planning, you should have ample time to draft, rewrite, proof, and polish a damn good paper. In the next chapter, I'll walk you through exactly what you need to do to write an awesome essay.

Honors and Awards

College applications have a section for you to list your scholastic achievement awards. You can list any achievement or honor you feel is appropriate. If you're in the Scouts, getting Eagle or Gold Star ranks are good ones to mention. Volunteer service awards are great, too. Don't limit yourself to just what you earned in school.

Extracurricular Activities

When I was going through school, parents, teachers, guidance counselors…everyone it seemed, emphasized how important extracurricular activities are in a college application. Well, yes and no.

Other activities can set you apart if you've got a solid academic transcript.

Maybe sports are your thing, or maybe you love volunteering in your community. Perhaps you belong to a church group, or you spend your spare time at the local soup kitchen.

Whatever your passion is, go after it. Get on the Internet and learn more about it. Educate yourself. Focus on a talent and hone it. The term "well rounded" is thrown around a lot, but that doesn't mean you have to get involved with everything.

There's a saying: jack-of-all-trades, master of none. If you spend all of your time divided among several activities, you'll never master any of them. Limit the scope of your activities, and spend your time developing your talents and passions rather than trying to get something else to put on your application.

Focusing your attention will also make it easier for you to earn some extra honors and recognition for your hard work.

Letters of Recommendation

Many schools require them, and many don't. Check to see what you need. Unlike your essay, these letters are the disinterested opinions of professional educators, so choose your mentors carefully.

Sometimes that choice will be made for you. For instance, your school may require a letter from your guidance counselor. If you're applying to a specialty school, like for engineering, they may require a letter from your most recent math teacher.

That's why you want to treat every teacher and administrator as if they are going to write your college recommendation letter. You don't want your dreams dashed because you were continually disruptive in one class (trust me).

Bear in mind that you are not the only student applying to college this year, so make sure to jump on those recommendation letters early. Find out who needs to write them as soon as possible and ask them. Remember that you're asking for a favor. They don't have to write anything for you, so be kind and ask if they wouldn't mind writing a recommendation. Often times, if you don't give them enough time, they won't be able to do it. I had a history teacher who had a sign in her class that said, "Poor planning on your part does not necessarily constitute an immediate emergency on my part." Translation: ask early.

If you get to select which teachers to pick, make sure to pick someone who knows you well, preferably has taught you in more than one class, and can speak well for your character and abilities. Don't go for the teacher that automatically gave you an A. Go for the one that knows you and can write well. Remember that they have to be persuasive and not everyone writes well, teachers included.

Also when asking, pay attention to your teacher's response. You want your teacher to say something like, "I'd be happy to" or "absolutely."

Any positive response given quickly bodes well for you. If, on the other hand, you sense any hesitation or resistance, excuse yourself by saying something like: "It's ok if you're busy. I have a few others already." You want shining recommendations, not half-hearted ones done out of a sense of guilt-driven obligation.

Once you get a yes, go one step further and provide your teacher with a résumé or a list of achievements. Your teachers may know you well, but that doesn't mean they remember everything you've done. Don't treat it like your teachers must mention everything you tell them (you're not writing the letter for them). Just present it and say something along the lines of, "I put together a list of my achievements just in case it's helpful to refer to something. I'd really appreciate it if you'd mention that I did [something], and again thank you for doing this." Teachers will appreciate this help because it's far easier to write a letter when you have some direction as opposed to coming up with something from scratch.

Ask for a few extra copies as well—more than just the applications you're sending out. That way, you won't have to bother your teacher for extra letters when you need them for other schools or scholarships. Provide them envelopes with stamps and addresses for each school you're applying to. Or you can ask for the letters in sealed envelopes with their signature across the flap. That way, you have several genuine copies whenever you need them, and if you have an extra, you can always peek if you're curious (but don't tell them you read it). Be sure to write a thank you letter to your teacher for their time and kind words. Write it, don't just say thanks and be done. Writing a letter means you were thinking about their generosity and made the effort to actually purchase a card and put it into writing. That means a lot more than just a verbal "thanks." They'll also remember your gratitude and may be more likely to help you out in the future.

For those of you that are going to a different school your senior year than the one you did for the past three, check to see if you can use letters from teachers at your old school. Look at the college's website, and if in doubt, call in and get that question answered. All the same rules still apply for asking early and being courteous.

Interviews

Not many colleges require interviews at all, but some offer them. I haven't run across any Universities that make admissions decisions based on interviews, but it might be good to have one to set yourself apart. If you're not comfortable, then there's no need to do one. An interview won't outweigh the rest of the application, but it can help put you over the top if you're close already.

If your choice school does require interviews, here are a few tips to get you through:

> If you have a solid application, an interview won't wreck it. One person's opinion of a 10-minute interaction with you won't overshadow years of hard work.

> It's ok to be nervous. Interviewers will expect you to be a little

nervous.

Dress like you're going to a job interview. It's better to be overdressed than underdressed.

Be honest. People can see when you're truly passionate about something. If they feel like you're lying, they won't trust you.

Presentation Tips

Many applications are done and submitted online now, but some may still require you to mail in a hard copy. If you happen to have to mail one in, or if you simply choose to, type as much of your application as possible. Don't hand-write your essay.

Make sure you have a professional looking email, like john.smith94@gmail.com instead of omggigglegurl96@yahoo.com. Yahoo, Gmail, and Outlook emails are all free, and you are allowed to have more than one. So there's no excuse to have a foolish looking email address on an important application.

And to drill it in one more time: start preparing your information now. Don't wait until the last minute. That way, you'll have all the time you need to make sure your application is the best it can be.

Chapter 5

How to Write a Stellar Essay

The essay is your chance to make your application more personal. Up until this point, you've been filling out answers to a form, but now you get to break free and do some writing. It's your chance to put your application over the top.

If you don't think you're a good writer, don't worry. In this chapter, I'm going to help you develop and refine your writing process so that your essay is the best it can be. I'll give you professional tips and practices that will not only help you rock the essay, but you'll also be able to take this skill with you into freshman comp and beyond.

There are two critical things you need to know about the Application essay. First is that it comes toward the end of the application. By the time an admissions reviewer gets to it, they've seen your transcript, honors, and activities. They might have even reviewed your recommendation letters already. In other words, the reviewer has some sense of what kind of student you are; now you have the opportunity to show what kind of person you are.

The second thing is that you need to pick a topic where you're struggling to keep under the word count limit. It's more difficult to write succinctly than it is to fill pages with words. Eliminate the fluff. Now, let's get started.

Most college essays are going to be between 250-650 words, and you'll likely be writing about a life experience you had or a justification as to why you're the sort of person that should go to your choice University.

Here are the theme choices from the 2015 Common App:

> Some students have a background or story that is so central to their identity that they believe their application would be incomplete without it. If this sounds like you, then please share your story.

> Recount an incident or time when you experienced failure. How did it affect you, and what lessons did you learn?

> Reflect on a time when you challenged a belief or idea. What prompted you to act? Would you make the same decision again?

> Describe a place or environment where you are perfectly content. What do you do or experience there, and why is it meaningful to you?

> Discuss an accomplishment or event, formal or informal, that marked your transition from childhood to adulthood within your culture, community, or family.

The essay can be tricky because you're writing about yourself. Strangely enough, that's not always easy to do. Remember to have confidence in your writing and in who you are. Write about what you know and not what you think the reviewer wants to read. You'll be more compelling.

Schedule, Pick, Plan, and Prepare

The worst thing you can do is put the essay off. Sure 650 words isn't much, but that's the challenge: how do you write something that stands out in a page and a half? The answer is simple—revisions. Plan to do at least 2 revisions on your own and have someone else proofread after that. The end result should feel like a crafted work rather than a short essay. To do that though, you need to plan it out and fit it into your already busy schedule.

Get out a calendar and schedule different times to work on the essay throughout the week. I'd recommend keeping your timeline short, say to 2 weeks maximum. A shorter deadline will keep you more focused on the work. Schedule these tasks on separate nights:

Pick a topic (30 mins)

Review other essays (1-1.5 hours)

Write the outline (1 hour)

Write the first draft (2-3 hours)

Write your first revision (2-3 hours)

Write your second revision (1-2 hours)

Have someone you trust proofread for you

Write the final draft (1 hour)

If you follow the task list, you should spend about 8-12 hours writing the essay, plus the wait time for someone else proofreading. The hours are just estimates meant to help you plan your schedule. You might not take as long or you might take a little longer, but if you take too much longer than 12 hours, you're overwriting.

Take the tasks and put them on your calendar. Make sure you block off enough time to accomplish everything, and be considerate of your proofreader's schedule too. Ask upfront if your proofreader is ok with helping you out, and then coordinate the hand-off and establish the expected turn around.

Pick a Topic

The essay themes are so broad that it should be easy to write upwards of 1,500 words. You might feel tempted to jump right in and start writing, but rather than start pounding the keys, pick the topic that you want. If you know right away, that's great. If you don't, not to worry: you only turn in the finished product. If you decide to write a different essay after you've already started one, that's fine.

The tricky part with the themes is that they're so general and broad. What you need to do is narrow down your subject. For example, you might choose the theme about failure. The topic will be narrower than the theme—something like losing first chair violin or not making the school basketball team. These are specific topics.

Picking a good topic is an art. Your essay can't be general; it's harder for a reader to feel connected to abstractions. Make your story concrete. People like action, conflict, and resolution. Your essay must have all three, and it must flow. All of this starts with the topic.

An example of something too broad would be writing about your entire freshman year. There are way too many events to include in a page and a half essay. Another example might be learning to cope with high school. You not only have to introduce the multitude of events to make sense of the topic, but you also have to tie them all together cogently. Again, this topic is too broad. Narrow it down.

Try thinking of a strong memory. You want to choose something that had an emotional impact on you. Analyze it and figure out what about that memory makes it so strong. Now ask yourself, is there action? Is there conflict? Is there a resolution? If so, it's a good place to start.

Avoid picking a topic that's predictable. A reader will glaze over something they've seen countless times before. Some overdone topics might include the death of an older relative, coming to grips with moving away from the place you grew up, or adjusting to a divorce in the family. These events are important to you and make you who you are, but a lot of students deal with the exact same issues. Unless you can approach them in a unique way, see if you can pick something else.

Try to pick something outside of school. If you had an amazing growth moment in 3rd period you simply must write about, write it—you're the author. Remember though that this is another place to demonstrate that you're involved outside of the classroom and have your own interests. Real life stories are more compelling.

Once you've got your topic in mind, jot down a few notes on how you plan to answer the questions. Break up the essay topic into its separate parts. You don't want to neglect answering one of the questions in the theme. These notes will eventually become an outline.

If you're absolutely drawing a blank for your topic, you can use some brainstorming techniques to figure out what you're going to write about. One is free writing. You put your pen to paper (or fingers to keys) and just start writing. They could be anything. They don't even have to be logical sentences or have punctuation. The point here is to get your momentum going. Don't stop and censor yourself. Write anything you want at first; then try to focus on something that was meaningful to you. Gently guide your writing toward your theme and see what comes out.

Mind mapping is another technique you can use. Summarize the theme up in one or two words in the center of the paper. Circle it and start drawing lines and bubbles from it. Write the first words that come to mind. As you branch out, you might hit something that pulls you in that direction. Draw more word bubbles branching off of that. Eventually, you'll have a big web of words and phrases, and in that loosely structured creative exercise, you might find the one word that inspires your topic.

If these feel too general and you want to focus your writing, find a piece you like, and start writing about the same topic. It could be an article in a newspaper, a blog, even a tweet. It doesn't matter where you find inspiration. Once you start writing something that comes easily to you, you'll find your mind more ready to work on an application essay.

You can try writing a letter to a friend and see where that takes you, or you can write an angry letter to a politician. Whatever inspires you at the time, get those fingers moving and the words flowing. Don't stop to think. Just keep moving.

Review Other Essays

At this point in your student career, you've written a lot of essays already. Many of them probably followed the 5-paragraph format or some other writing guide. I'd urge you to avoid falling back on a pre-determined format. They tend to be boring and predictable. You want something that stands out and breaks away from everyone else's style. Finding good examples of successful college essays is a good start.

If you have older siblings in college, ask to see their admissions essays. Go online and look for examples. Improving your familiarity with what a good admissions essay looks like will help you more than you know.

The challenge is to make sure you don't inadvertently copy that style. Try to get at what makes the essay interesting. Focus on the emotions you feel when you read the essay. That's what makes something relatable. Use other works for inspiration, not as a style guide.

Write the Outline

Now that you've got a good grasp on your topic and have seen good examples of finished products, it's time to outline your essay.

Take your notes from when you were picking a theme and flesh them out a little. Do your outline in bullet points. This makes it easy for you to move things around and rearrange a little if you have to. Remember that a good story has action, conflict, and resolution. Start your outline with those points. Here is an example of my outline when I applied to grad school:

Theme: Why do you want to get a Wake Forest MBA?

Topic: How I came to live in North Carolina, decide to get an MBA, and pick Wake Forest.

- Introduction
  - Didn't know I ever wanted an MBA
    - Join Navy
    - Odd jobs traveling
    - Fishing in Argentina

- o How I came to live in North Carolina
  - ▪ Unpredicted
- Turning Point
  - o Having a family
  - o Getting hired at a design agency
  - o Emphasize progress despite struggle
- Why an MBA
  - o Further my business knowledge
  - o Further my career
- Why Wake Forest
  - o Reputation
  - o Faculty – Dean of Business School, Steve Reinemund
- Conclusion
  - o Benefits
    - ▪ Put knowledge to action in real time
    - ▪ Gain knowledge to run business

Action points:

- Move to NC
- Take job at design agency

- Build business

Conflict:

- Hard economy

- Unforeseen career path

Resolution:

- Getting an MBA

The outline is broken up, first by how I wanted the essay to flow and second to make sure I had action, conflict, and resolution. As you can see, even in something as cut and dry as an MBA application essay, you can find a compelling story.

Write and Revise

Now it's time to start typing up your essay. With your outline in hand, you should have a pretty quick time of it. First drafts are not perfect, and they never will be. Not even professionals get it right on the first draft.

As a writer, I had a hard time with this concept for a while. It wasn't until I chose to write a book that I learned it was ok to be terrible on the first draft. Just start typing from your outline, and let the words come. Sure some of them will seem like mindless drivel, but that's ok. First drafts are always garbage. The most important thing is to write.

As you write your essay, you might stop for a minute to think and reread what you've written. Something seems a little out of place so you make a quick edit. Now you see a comma splice, and you fix that too. Next you see a phrase you don't quite like, and so you spend more time thinking about a better way to write what you've already written. This process is called Editing, and he's a pushy SOB. He pops in when you should be focusing on writing and distracts you from getting done what you need to get done.

Your job is to make sure to keep editing in his place – after the rough draft is written. Editing is all about improving what you have, which is impossible if what you have is an unfinished draft, so don't waste time editing what you've written until you're done writing.

As a writer, you must accept the fact that your first draft of anything is going to be crap. Don't expect perfection on the first pass, and don't waste time trying to achieve it there. That's why there are drafts. Give yourself permission to write badly. The whole point is to slowly hone your writing in manageable phases and not worry about the final essay until you're to that step. Drafts are the method by which your vision and your writing will meet.

Unfortunately, I didn't save my first draft of the application essay to share, but rest assured that it wasn't that interesting.

First Revision

The first revision is always the biggest one. Here you want to focus a lot on flow, voice, and tone. Leave the word-smithing until the end.

Make sure you address the following questions:

> Does this sound like me? Is it my voice?

> Does this essay flow logically? Can I go from one paragraph to the next without getting lost?

> Does my impact match my intent? — This is a concept I ran into in business school. The idea is that any action you take has an intended outcome. The outcome you desire is your intent. How other people react to your actions is the impact. If their reactions are aligned with what you had wanted, then your intent matched your impact.

> Am I answering the provided theme? — Ask this one during every revision.

Once you're comfortable with the bulk of the essay, you've finished your first revision. Remember, you're concentrating on major pieces like structure and flow. You'll probably have a good amount of rewriting to do, but don't agonize over word choice just yet. The key here is structure.

As you revise, don't be surprised if you move whole paragraphs around. Something at the end may be more dramatic at the beginning. Remember, you want action and conflict to pull your reader in. Often times, writers will start stories in media res, or in the middle of things. Even if your essay isn't chronological, it must flow logically.

Is there action? One way to improve flow and increase action is to use active voice. In an active voice construction, the actor does something as opposed to passive voice where something is done upon the actor.

> Lisa slammed the door on Karl's foot. – Active. Lisa is slamming the door.

> The door was slammed on Karl's foot by Lisa. – Passive. The door was acted upon by someone else, but we don't know who until the end of the sentence. In fact, you can remove Lisa entirely and the sentence still makes sense.

> The door was slammed on Karl's foot. Now Lisa got away with slamming the door on poor Karl without anyone taking notice. Removing the actor removes the responsibility and the blame. Passive voice also reads slow and complicates sentence structure.

The nature of revising makes it hard to divide them into discrete pieces. You'd think you'd just keep editing until you have a finished product, but it's easier to focus on one piece at a time. This means breaking up how you approach each revision. The trick is knowing when you've finished. Here is a good test for your first revision:

Read through the essay. If you don't get tripped up reading it and you feel you've made a strong point, then you're good to move on.

Second Revision

Step away from the essay for a few days and come back to it for the second revision. At this point you shouldn't have to rewrite too much. Now you want to see if there are better ways to say what you've said.

The first thing I do in a second revision is cut out unnecessary words. If you're like me, you have heavily Latinized writing. By that I mean you use a lot of prepositions and longer words when you could be using shorter ones. I certainly don't advocate dumbing down your writing, but I will say there's a trade-off with word choice.

English is a rich language. It's full of many words that evoke different images even though the definitions are similar. For example joy and rapture both mean happy, but their impacts are slightly different in a reader's mind. Happy is a boring word because it's overused. Joy might draw up images of a person smiling from ear to ear. Rapture is more of an uncontrolled and almost debilitating state of happiness, like euphoria. Each of these words has its proper place in writing. For example, saying someone is "elated" is far more descriptive than saying "very happy."

That all being said, you can go over the top with long words. For example, I'd probably go with, "I am terrified of long words" rather than "I have hippopotomonstrosesquipedaliophobia."

Another candidate for the chopping block are the phrases, "I think," "I believe," and "It is my opinion that." Introductions like that not only take away from the number of words you can use, but they also weaken your tone.

Examine the difference between these two sentences:

I believe that anyone who is interested should be able to attend college.

Anyone should be able to attend college.

The second sentence is not only shorter, it is stronger. You are the author of your essay, so the reader assumes everything is your opinion (unless it's a cited fact). There's no need to qualify everything with "I believe." Have conviction in what you say. Remove weak modifiers, such as, "kind of," "sort of," "seemed," and "appeared to." It's like you're trying to say something without consequence; in turn, your writing will be without consequence, and in the writing world, that is real failure. Take a stand.

Look out for prepositions, too. Prepositions exist solely to describe one word's relationship to the next. Water and bucket for example. There's water in the bucket. "In" tells you the relationship between water and bucket, nothing else. Prepositions are absolutely necessary, but too many of them means there are fewer nouns and verbs. Nouns and verbs are critical because they carry the action and tell the story. Also look for words like "that." You can usually find a way to get rid of it.

Remove qualifiers and adverbs as much as possible—you've got a word limit after all. Words like "very" are always unnecessary. Choose an adjective that has the magnitude you want. For instance, "very mad" would be better as "furious." Also remember some words don't use qualifiers. Words like "perfect, unique," and "true" don't have degrees.

Nothing is more unique or truer than something else; they can be only unique or true.

If you do need to use qualifiers, make sure you place them correctly. "Only" is a common candidate for being in the wrong place. Most people put it before the verb when speaking: "I only want a new pair of shoes." Everyone would get that the speaker wants only a new pair of shoes—not the literal meaning that the only action the speaker takes is to want the new shoes. In print, "only" should immediately precede the word it modifies. Here are some examples:

> "My mother has only five children." This means that mother has five children, which by implication isn't a large amount in the context of the sentence.

> "My mother only has five children." This means that dear old mother possesses nothing else but her five children.

> "My only mother has five children." This means that my mother is my only one.

> "Only my mother has five children." This means nobody else has five children.

> "My mother has five only children." Though not technically accurate, this could be an ironic statement meant to describe the lack of relationship between the five children.

Scan your writing for sentences that are unclear and confusing. They need to be fixed. One way to make your writing clearer is to use specific names. For example, rather than saying "my math teacher," introduce her as "Mrs. Cockrell." Readers connect with names. Another way you can sharpen your writing is to remove vague reference wherever possible.

Vague reference happens when you start sentences with empty pronouns like "it" and demonstratives like "there." Everyone violates this rule from time to time. My take on it is that if a reader gets what you're saying without getting tripped up, you're fine. If a reader doesn't get what you're referring to, that's vague reference.

Every sentence must have a reason to be on the page. Look for any asides that are unrelated to the point of the story. For instance something like this: "My mother, who was tired from aerobics class, offered to help me with my math homework." Do we need to know your mother was tired? If so, do we need to know it was from aerobics class? Imagine yourself as a surgeon with a scalpel. Rid your essay of the extra fat.

Once you're satisfied with your revisions, it's time to listen to what you wrote. Read your essay aloud, and don't be shy or nervous about talking to an empty room; plenty of people do it because it's a great way to hear how your essay will read. If something is off, unclear, or cluttered, your ear will pick it up right way—a lot faster than your eyes could.

If you have to read your essay a couple of times, go for it. You should work until you're satisfied. Your speech should flow naturally. If you get at the end of a sentence and find you're out of breath, chances are the sentence is too long. If you forget what a sentence is about as you say it, it's too long. Keep in mind that reading won't catch everything. Reading helps with flow and structure, but you won't hear the difference between a comma and a semi-colon.

You're going to want a great, crisp essay that reflects all the reasons why you should get admitted to your school of choice. You need to prove that you belong in that college. So you want to make sure your essay is the best it can be. Make any changes you need to.

Hopefully these tips help you do the craftwork involved with your second revision. To use an archaeology metaphor, if you're first revision is a shovel, moving large piles of dirt around, then your second revision is a brush, slowly revealing the final picture.

More Writing Tips

As you write, try to keep these things in mind, and you'll have a stellar essay. Rule number one is always be yourself. Don't write something you think colleges want to see. They want to see you. A genuine story is the most important thing. The rest is polish.

Be different. Large colleges get much more than 10,000 applications each year, and they all come in between January and April. Reviewers have to move quickly through a lot of applications, so you want to catch their attention quickly and differentiate yourself.

You're fighting for attention. You want that hazy, bleary-eyed reviewer to sit up and forget the coffee she was reaching for. You want to be interesting. Interesting writing comes from the heart. Don't write just to take up space. Empty words on a page are no different than empty words from someone's mouth. They lack substance, purpose, and captivation. You don't want your reader's eyes to glaze over.

I alluded to this before, but I want to bring it up again: don't inflate your language because you think it sounds more sophisticated. It doesn't. Another symptom of Latinized writing is having too many nouns. Use verbs instead. People like action. Your goal should be to remove as many superfluous words as possible.

I understand: it's hard to pare down your message and get excited about an application essay, but you have to find some way to get passionate about it. It will show through naturally in your word choice. Your essay will go from being academic and long-winded to conversational and warm. That's what people will relate to.

Your writing has to have substance, which means you have to believe in it, and it has to be you. You might be funny, clever, and confident—let these show through in your writing. Don't just mechanically manufacture an essay and expect to stand out. Don't be afraid to joke around. Honestly, if you get marks off for showing a little personality, do you really want to go to that school anyway?

You want your content to be compelling and memorable; however, you also want it readable, and that means knowing grammar, spelling, and syntax. Another thing you'll want to do is vary your sentence length. Short sentences are powerful. Use them to emphasize a point, but too many short sentences makes writing choppy. Longer sentences allow you to convey more complex ideas that can't be summed up in a few words. If all of your sentences are long though, you'll exhaust the reader and lose her attention. That's why you need to vary sentence length.

Don't take too long to make your point. When looking at sentence structure, count how many words come before your verb. If your subject is too long, your readers might forget what's going on. People need action to pay attention. Things aren't interesting unless they do something. Rocks for example, not so interesting by themselves, but place them snugly in David's slingshot, and we've got ourselves a story.

Make sure to use your punctuation correctly. Punctuation helps pace the reader and divides up complete thoughts. Poor punctuation exhausts the reader, and it makes your writing look childish. Use more than commas. Learn how to use colons, semicolons, dashes, and parentheses. Remember, run-on sentences are nobody's friend.

Aside from simple grammatical edits like spelling and comma splices, look for higher-level mistakes like dangling and misplaced modifiers. Can you spot the problems in the following sentences?

> "Driving through the street, the car started to shake." The car is not doing the driving, you are. Make sure the subject of the main clause is someone that can actually drive.

"I saw your friend while playing basketball." Who was playing basketball? While playing basketball, I saw your friend or I saw your friend while he was playing basketball.

Try not to be overly emotional in your essay, and don't overuse exclamation points! Avoid grandiose statements about how life as you knew it was over. This is called hyperbole. Hyperbole can be humorous and effective when used correctly, but you're describing something that's near and dear to you. If you're truly passionate about a topic, your writing will reflect that naturally.

Avoid clichés at all costs. Overused metaphors don't require much thought, and they aren't exciting. Read George Orwell's essay, *Politics in the English Language*. It's an incredible argument against using euphemism and passive voice in writing and speech. Though his essay is politically motivated, Orwell makes a valid point, and all writers should heed it: when you use someone else's words, you're letting that person do the thinking for you. What results is writing that is unoriginal, uninspiring, and unremarkable.

I'm not saying you have to coin a new phrase at each new paragraph. Nobody expects that. I am saying to use words you know and words that work. Demonstrate how much thought and effort you put into your writing. One way to do that is to develop well thought out analogies, but try to stick to one analogy in the essay if you can. When you start off with something like "I felt like a captain of a ship," keep using nautical metaphors. Don't switch it up to trains or something.

Be vivid. Describe the scenes before you with enough detail to let the reader see your story. After that, let them fill in the blanks. Don't get hung up on details that don't matter. For example: "The building was made of red brick, at least 30 feet high. It smelled like turpentine, which could be explained by the janitor in the corner in his blue jumpsuit. He was still mopping the floor, back and forth, back and forth." Unless there's something critical, we can drop a lot of the detail here. People have seen brick buildings and know what they look like. People have seen janitors and can picture them too. All you really need is to say the building was brick, tall, and smelled of turpentine. Something like "The brick façade towered over us. The scent of turpentine seared our nostrils."

Avoid summing up at the end. Let the events speak for themselves. Don't end with something like, "And that's how I learned to be more tolerant, a trait which will serve me well in college." Or, "And that's how I came to appreciate my family. They are always there for me." There are no blockbuster movies where at the end, the director comes on screen and tells you the importance of what just happened. Give readers credit. They're smart enough to figure out that stuff.

Remember, you want to tell a story about yourself, but don't use the essay as a platform for self-aggrandizement. Focus on the action and the conflict. There are other places on the application to list your accomplishments but not here. Just tell the story.

The most enjoyable stories are where the speaker has an authentic voice.

Readers are consumers of thought, and they behave like every other consumer—through emotion. Yes, the college admissions officer has to read your essay, but that doesn't mean they'll like what you've written. You want to make their decision an easy one. To do that, you should know there are two types of decisions: emotional ones and logical ones. Most decisions are actually emotional, which are later justified with logic. Emotional decisions are made almost on the spot. Logical decisions take time to carefully weigh all options.

You want an emphatic yes, not a long and calculated one. Strong convictions are exclusively emotional, so you need your reader to connect with what you have to say. The only way to do that is to let you and your passion shine through. You can't fake good writing.

I know this feels like a lot to take in, but keep your spirits up. Writing is a difficult process; most of it is a mental battle you must overcome time and time again. By now you may be sick of your essay. You may wish you never had to look at it again but have the painful knowledge that you will. This is why good planning rocks. You can afford to walk away and refresh your brain. When you come back, find something you like about your writing. Hold on to that feeling and let it fuel you to move forward. Look in the mirror and say things like, "You're going to do this." "You're doing so well." "You'll definitely get in." Get revved up and go. After all, you can do this.

Proofread and Final Draft

Now your essay should be at the point where you'd feel good about submitting it, but before you do, make sure to have someone else proofread it. All of the best writers also have great editors that peruse and critique their work until they have a finished product. The essay might be great as is, but you have author's bias. You know what your intent is, so it's impossible to know what the impact will be until others tell you.

For your proofreader, pick someone whose perspective you respect and who's comfortable being brutally honest with you. Your proofreader may come back and say that you should do a lot of rewrites. You may have to go back to revising. Make sure you trust the person giving you that advice. On the other hand, you don't want someone telling you your work is great when it isn't. You need honesty.

Final Tweaks

Once you have your feedback, go and implement as much of it as you think necessary. After all, you are the author and the only one responsible for the quality of your essay. If you disagree with a comment your proofreader made, seek a second opinion or just submit the essay as is.

Here is the final version of my grad school essay:

> If you had asked me a few years ago what I'd be pursuing now, an MBA would not have been my first response. I would have

talked about how I was going join the Navy and see the world. I may have mentioned spending a few years traveling and taking odd jobs for subsistence. At one point, I even considered contracting myself on a fishing vessel out of Argentina just to improve my Spanish and get a chance to see Antarctica. But the events in my life brought me to North Carolina in 2009, blessed me with two daughters, and started me down a path I could have never predicted. I call that Providence.

In June of 2010, my mentor and future father-in-law, René Rodriguez, hired me as a project manager for his scrappy branding agency in Kernersville. His offer surprised me because I had no background in branding or project management, but I threw myself into the role.

Over the past two years, René and I built up the business and can now boast a client list that includes Jeff Foxworthy, Harvard University, Magellan Health Services, and Six Flags. Our internal staff tripled during that time too, and all this during the worst recession in living memory.

Progress did not come easily. We achieved only through tireless drive, sacrifice, and enough coffee to drown an elephant. We built a culture centered on the idea that Fortune favors the Brave, and there's nothing brave about standing still in business.

My decision to pursue an MBA seemed only logical; I just had to find the right institution. If I've learned nothing else, it's that reputation is everything. That's why I started looking at Wake Forest. Though I considered other programs, I found everything I needed in the Winston-Salem Evening MBA.

As I dug deeper into the school and its philosophies, I knew it was for me. I was drawn to the caliber and quality of the faculty. I read more about Steve Reinemund and his climb from wage worker at Roy Rogers to CEO of PepsiCo. He's a man that understands business from all levels, and he chose to be at Wake Forest. My choice was clear.

Rhino Graphica is still growing, and I must evolve further to be an effective leader. While studying for an MBA, I'll be able to put what I learn into practice the next day, and my experience will enhance my understanding for the next class. Eventually the company will open a second office, and I'll need the skills and wherewithal to run it myself.

As I gain experience and expertise, I'll one day run the entire agency, most likely in addition to other companies I plan to start. If I want to reach that height in my career, I have to take the surest steps to get there. From what I've read and researched, an MBA from Wake Forest is a sure thing.

Formatting

The last thing you should do is format your essay. Word is particularly picky, and it will try to auto-format a lot of your work. Take some time to learn how to format in Word (it's a great skill to have), and apply your changes to your final draft.

To make sure you're using good formatting practices: use consistent headings, make sure paragraph spacing is equal, ensure indentations are applied properly, add page numbers for multi-page essays, etc. These are the small touches that can make the difference between amateur and professional. You'll have to learn formatting sometime soon if you haven't already.

Once you're satisfied, send off the application. Don't let it sit around because it will keep bothering you in the back of your mind. You need to get focused on the next thing, not constantly revisit something that's already done.

If you feel nervous about the essay, that's ok. It's natural. Good writing takes time and commitment. Honestly, I didn't take my writing seriously until I got to college. High school writing just seemed so formulaic. Write your intro paragraph, support it with three more paragraphs, cite your evidence, and conclude. Bleh. I even had teachers say they hated the 5-paragraph format, but our classes were subject to the state curriculum. I never truly learned the value of revision or style because the scoring rubrics focused more on my facts being correct and my conclusions being logical. I don't blame teachers so much as the system.

As I researched essays for this book, I came across so many that were genuinely good reads. I couldn't remember if my style was any good back then. Curiosity got the best of me, so I started digging around and found an old scholarship essay. It read more like a bad marketing piece than a personal narrative. Nobody is born knowing these things, and had I sought to improve my writing back then, I would have written a much more engaging essay, and I may have won more scholarship money.

PART 2: CONQUERING COLLEGE

Getting this far is no easy feat, so congratulations! It's tough work picking out a school and putting the application together, but once you've been accepted, there's no feeling quite like it. The next few years of your life are going to be great, but it will be hard work. If college isn't hard for you, then you're not getting what you're paying for. Challenge yourself. That's what this time in life is about.

College has an entirely different dynamic than high school. There's more responsibility, and therefore more accountability. You won't have weekly assignments or daily homework. Instead, your entire grade for the semester might ride on as few as two exams and a paper. There's less chance to catch up if you miss an assignment.

Amid your studies, you might decide to get an internship, join a sports team, or become part of a social group. You'll have a lot more freedom and time to balance, and you won't have a daily routine, which makes it easier to forget and miss things.

Then there are the finances! Not only do you have tuition and books to worry about, you'll have other needs to pay for. You'll need to create a budget, and if you plan to buy a car, you'll need to learn how to develop your credit early on.

Not to worry, the next part of this book will walk you through some efficiency hacks to help you get the biggest return on your study time with less effort. I'll also share some tips on how to create budgets you can live with, how to build your credit (including what types of cards to apply for), and where to find some last-minute college money.

Chapter 6

Free Money and How to Pay For School

The next few years of your life are going to be fun, challenging, and hectic. For many families, the biggest struggle is the financing. There are four basic ways to get money for college: grants, scholarships/contests, loans, and wages.

In this chapter, I'll explain each of these in more detail. I'll provide loads of resources for you to check out and some tips on how to manage it all. Pay close attention to this chapter because free money is good money.

Grants

Grants are free money given from the government, both federal and state, to help defray the cost of qualified college expenses. Whether or not you receive a grant is based on a variety of factors, and there are different types of grants with varying requirements.

When awarding grants, the government takes into account your academic qualifications, your financial need, your ability to pay for school, and your current status. Generally, there are need-based grants and merit-based grants. In order to get considered, you have to file a Free Application for Federal Student Aid (FAFSA). The deadline to file the FAFSA is early in the year, usually around February, so make sure to check out their website (http://www.fafsa.ed.gov) sooner rather than later. You'll need to have your primary guardian's tax return, and you'll have to fill it out every year you plan to attend school.

A note for the young men: you cannot get federal aid if you're not registered with the Selective Service. You have to register before your 18th birthday, and they'll give you an SSS number. Hang on to it, as you'll need it for certain legal forms. Women don't have to worry about registering. Go to http://www.sss.gov to register and learn more.

There are also grants for minority students, women, and those with disabilities. There are grants for art students, engineering students, environmental studies, journalism, law, math, medicine, nursing, physical therapy, social work, teaching, and more.

Many of these grants also count your Expected Family Contribution (EFC), the number of members in your family, including other dependents, and family assets. They also account for your ability to pay.

Colleges expect that a higher percentage of your money (about a third) is going to college expenses. They estimate your parents will contribute around 5% of their earned income. You should know that colleges will look at your parents' 1040 tax returns for your senior year, meaning that any big bumps in income would be best put off until after December 31st of that year. Although you will need your parents' tax returns, you can file the FAFSA and use an estimate based on the previous year. This is pretty easy to do for most salaried employees. Contractors and freelancers with sporadic income will have a harder time. In those cases, estimate a conservative income. A lot of grant money is first-come, first-served, and they are generally need-based. Don't outright lie in your estimates; aside from being unethical, you'll have to go back and update the FAFSA once your parents file their taxes. Just take advantage of whatever reasonable leeway you have.

Also, if you don't update your FAFSA, your application may undergo verification, which means you'll need to provide documents to support the income figures you put. Verification could mean a delay in getting your financial aid.

Once your FAFSA is done, I'd recommend sitting down with your parents to help calculate your Expected Family Contribution. Collegetoolkit.com has a good calculator to help you figure out the EFC: http://calculators.collegetoolkit.com/college-calculators/rescalcefc.aspx

Grants are often awarded automatically, but make sure to research anyway. There may be different opportunities between your home state and your college's state (if they're different). See if there is some information you need to include to qualify.

Scholarships

There are several types of scholarships. Not all of them are academic based, so even if you don't have the best grades, it's worth checking out what's available.

The first place to start is with your high school. Talk to your guidance counselor and see if there are any scholarships available. You might find out about a few local ones that you can apply to. They might range from $250-$2000.

Never turn down a scholarship opportunity because the prize isn't a whopping five figures. Small amounts add up, and competition is usually less stiff. Going to college with $1,500 of free money is still better than $0.

The second place to go is the financial aid office at your college. They might say that you are automatically considered from your FAFSA submission, but there might be a few that aren't automatically applied. Look up your University's Financial Aid office and shoot them an email. Try to set up an in-person visit if possible.

Another good idea is to send letters to your state government officials. Send letters to the governor, state delegates, state senators, federal senators, and federal representatives. The worst thing they can say is there is nothing available.

In these letters, make sure you include your GPA, your goals, what you plan to do with your education, your financial situation, and your contributions to your community.

Finally, take to the web and search for scholarships. Here are a few resources to check out (links listed in Appendix C for reference):

CollegeScholarships.org has a lot of great information on scholarships of all sorts, including athletic, minority, by state, and by chosen major.

FastWeb.com is a free service that has you enter in information about yourself, and it shows you available scholarships based on it. You can sort by deadline or prize amount.

Scholarships.com works similarly to FastWeb. Just fill out a free profile, and you'll get matched with relevant scholarships.

Finaid.org has even more great ideas on financial aid help. Be sure to see the prestigious scholarships section for a list of national scholarship providers. It also has information on loans and military aid.

Collegeboard.org is the source for SAT and AP class information, but it also has a book list for ways on how to finance college, including a Scholarship Handbook with more than 2,000 programs listed.

Scholarshipexperts.com lists several available scholarships as well as some of their own. Some of the subject choices include "I Have a Dream," "Make Me Laugh," and "Zombie Apocalypse."

Knowhow2go.acenet.edu is geared towards high school students and military veterans alike. In addition to useful aid information, there are helpful guides on exploring interests and success stories.

Of course, you can always search for scholarships on Google, but be careful. There are plenty of scams out there, so before you submit any personal information, make sure you trust the source. Here are a few ways you can make sure the site is legit:

If the website looks like a toddler put it together, steer clear. Legitimate sites will try to at least look legitimate. Don't trust anything that looks like a tumblr blog.

Try searching for reviews of the websites you find. Someone else may have had a bad experience. Remember though that some people badmouth legitimate Websites for whatever reason, and not all reviews are accurate. If the reviews are overwhelmingly negative, that's a good sign you don't want to get involved.

When in doubt, look for accreditation badges on the website, such as the Better Business Bureau or TRUSTe. You can usually find these in the website's privacy policy. If the site doesn't have a privacy policy, then you have no business giving them any information about you.

Anything with .gov or .edu in the URL is safe. Those types of domains have to be registered and verified before they're allowed to go up.

If you do happen to find something on the Web and are not quite sure if it's legit, visit www.ftc.gov/scholarshipscams.

The FTC (Federal Trade Commission) hires professional watchdogs that make sure U.S. businesses operate within the law, which means honestly representing who you are; however, scams still pop up quickly before the FTC can shut them down.

You can always ask your friends to see if they have any experience with a questionable site.

To give you a better idea of the range of what's out there, I've put together a list of a few national scholarships you can look into:

The Coca-Cola Scholars Foundation offers several million dollars in scholarship money. They have various programs and applications. Their Scholars Program is open to all high-school students not affiliated with the company. Their All-State Community College Academic Team Program provides stipends to current community college students. Visit their site for more information on these programs, who is eligible, and when to apply.

Best Buy also offers scholarships open to all high school students. You can view more information on the cappex.com website.

Buick has the Buick Achievers Program. All this money for a few pieces of paper!

Sallie Mae is one of the biggest lenders for students. Interestingly enough, they also have a search tool on their site for grants and scholarships.

One of the richest men in the world also happens to be one of the biggest philanthropists. The Bill & Melinda Gates Foundation in conjunction with the United Negro College Fund has set up the Gates Millennium Scholars Program, which gives away 1,000 scholarships each year to minority students.

Ronald McDonald House Charities also offers different scholarships. These are offered from their local branches usually.

Tylenol has its own set of scholarships with 10 applicants receiving $10,000 and 30 getting $5,000 each.

You can also find countless scholarships based on heritage, sports you played, and places you lived. You might also want to see if any big local businesses in your community offer anything. Many times, companies have a "public good-will budget" which means they have a certain amount of money they give to the community each year. Find a company that gives frequently and ask if they ever thought of offering a scholarship. The worst answer you'll get is no.

Companies sometimes offer educational assistance to their employees. General Electric, for example, has a GE Star Awards program for employee's children attending college. So ask a parent to find out about these types of programs at work. You never know.

Several community groups like the Rotary Club, the Elks Club, the Lion's Club, and many more offer scholarships through their local chapters. Reach out and get information about them.

Also consider what communities you belong to. The National Eagle Scout Association offers merit-based scholarships to Eagle Scouts from across the country. In 2015, they'll offer around 250 scholarships ranging from $1,000 to $50,000. I'd say that's worth a look.

States also offer assistance in return for you working for a number of years after graduation. For instance, future educators can get money from the state to pay for college in return for working in the education field for some years immediately following graduation. These are contracts you take out with the state, and there are big penalties for not following through on your part of the bargain. If you're dead sure of your commitment, then these are great opportunities; however, if you're not sure about what you want to study, you not only have decided your major, you have also signed the next few years of your life away. Do so with caution.

Another thing to keep in mind is that you can apply to scholarships every year. Many are available for college students as well as high school students. Don't think that you apply once and that's the end of it, unless of course you hate free money.

Contests

In addition to merit-based scholarships, there are also contests that award money for college. The great thing about these is that they can play to your other strengths, giving you the chance to stand out more.

Ever want to get paid to do a book report? Check out aynrand.org. There are more than 600 prizes valued at $99,000 in scholarship money for essay contests on Ayn Rand's books. All you have to do is read one of her books, and write a great essay on it. With any luck, you'll win some cash.

Love public speaking? Then the American Legion Oratorical Contest might be for you. The top prize is $18,000 for the national winner and $1,500 to whoever makes it into the first round. Get your speech chops ready.

Is science your passion? Then the DuPont Challenge is a good place to start. In 2015, they're hosting a science essay competition, and the essay is only 1,000 words long (that's 2-3 pages)!

Every year, the National History Day Contest gathers the best and brightest students to discuss a common passion: dead people. Contest winners can receive scholarships as well!

If you're an advocate of peace, then you might want to check out the National Peace Day Contest. Enter an award-winning essay, and get free money.

Prudential Spirit of Community Awards honors students that make a difference in their communities. Awards range from $1,000 to $5,000, and it's not bad to add to a college application either.

If you want something a bit more on the creative side, take a look at the

Scholastic Art and Writing Awards. Entries range from creative writing pieces, to sculpture, photography, and oil canvas.

Are you a tech junkie? Check out the Toshiba/NSTA ExploraVision contest. You can imagine what technology will look like in 20 years and maybe get paid for your vision.

The American Museum of Natural History also hosts the Young Naturalist Awards each year for students that are passionate about ecology and the natural sciences.

As you can see, there are plenty of opportunities available.

Loans

Hopefully you're able to defray tuition with grants and scholarships, but a lot of scholarships don't cover room and board (though some do). To make up the difference, it's common to take out student loans.

On the one hand, student loans tend to have lower rates and are a good way to start building your credit, but they can also add up and be difficult to payoff. You have to weigh your options carefully and determine how much in loans you want to take versus pay yourself. It's becoming increasingly difficult for students to begin their loan repayments so soon after college. At that point, the monthly payment will most likely be a large percentage of your income.

There are different types of student loans you can go after. The most common loan is the Stafford Loan. This money comes directly from the Federal government and can be subsidized or unsubsidized.

In a subsidized loan, you don't pay the interest on the loan while you're in school, the government does. This helps save a lot of money since you won't be getting hit with interest on interest. This type of scholarship is for families that can demonstrate financial hardship. The maximum amount you can borrow is $23,000.

In an unsubsidized loan, interest starts accruing as soon as you borrow. This means you'll pay interest accruing on interest.

Perkins Loans are also popular, but they are reserved for students with financial need. Although the government funds these loans, the schools determine who should get them (they have a limited amount to disburse each year). These loans generally have lower interest rates.

PLUS Loans are for parents and grad students. These have higher interest rates, but they can be used to cover things like room and board.

To apply for government-funded loans, you'll need to fill out the FAFSA. To expedite the FAFSA application process, register for a PIN so you can fill it out online; otherwise, you have to mail it in, and that takes longer to process.

There are also private education loans. These come from banks rather than the government and are based on your family's credit-worthiness. Although terms vary by lender, be wary of private loans. Repayment tends to be less flexible. Whereas you may be able to extend deferment or apply for economic hardship on government-funded loans once you graduate, private banks are less likely to be as accommodating.

Here are some additional resources regarding loans for you to check out:

Loan Repayment Calculator:

http://calculators.collegetoolkit.com/college-calculators/rescalcloan.aspx

General Financial Aid information:

http://www.savingforcollege.com

Information on Federal Loans:

https://studentaid.ed.gov/resources

Information on types of student loans:

http://www.debt.org/students/types-of-loans/

Wages

Even if your scholarships and grants only get you part of the way, you can also opt to pay the difference with money you earn. Money paid for college is tax deductible up to $4,000. You'll get a 1098-T form from your school at the beginning of each year to file with your taxes, so make sure to get that.

Since tax law is subject to change, visit http://www.irs.gov for the latest tax information.

The most ideal way to pay for college is with scholarships and grants. The benefits of paying with wages over taking out loans are that you come out with no debt, and you don't pay any interest.

Military

If you're going the Military route, you'll need to talk to your recruiter about what programs are available to you. All branches offer great incentives for you to get your degree, and the best part is, you can get an education for free. Visit http://www.students.gov to find out more about how the military can help you in your college career. If you don't want to go full active duty, you can join the reserves or the National Guard.

So now you have a pretty clear idea of the different ways you can pay for college. Make sure to get as many grants and scholarships as you can. There are a lot of scholarships that offer recurring payments, and you can keep applying to scholarships each year. There are fewer to choose from once you're in college, but they do exist. Spending your time finding and getting scholarships will give you a better return than a minimum wage job, so think of it as your job.

Chapter 7

Preparing for the First Day

Getting ready for school is exciting. It's a new time in your life, and you'll have a lot more freedom and choices to make. College isn't just about classes. There's community, living circumstances, and the logistics of becoming independent. In this chapter we'll look at the major milestones you might encounter and must-know tips on how to navigate the lesser-discussed truths about college life.

Housing

Housing can be a tricky thing, but it's also very exciting. The problem with choosing your housing as a freshman is that you're low on the totem pole. You have to vie with other students for the best spots, especially on campus. Some colleges will require that you live on campus for the first year, but then again, you might not have to. You'll put in a housing application and request where you want to live. If they let you recommend roommates, you have to decide who you're going to room with. Remember that this isn't a guarantee; you live wherever they tell you, but for the most part, colleges do their best to be as accommodating as possible. If, for example, they pair you with someone you end up not being able to live with, it will cost them time and money to relocate you, not to mention you'll have to repack everything. So it's in their best interest to place you where you're more likely to get along.

Once you know what kind of room you'll be staying in, you'll have to plan to pack appropriately. This will be infinitely easier if you've seen the freshman dorms beforehand. Plan a trip back out to campus with your family and take a good hard look at the dorms. In your first visit, you might not have been sure this was the college for you, but now you'll have a different perspective because you know you'll be attending.

For your first few years, I'd recommend living on campus, and here's why:

College is about expanding your horizons, both educationally and experientially. You're going to meet new people. There's always something going on around campus, and the fact that your living space is so close to your classes really helps you out. Not to mention, parking is limited, and a lot of universities don't allow freshmen to park on campus, which means if you get an apartment in town, you'll have to ride with someone else or take the bus in.

On top of that, colleges are set up to be social. Everyone in the dorm is about your age; some are probably in your classes. You'll be living near a common building where everyone hangs out. If you're off campus, your neighbors might not be students; you'll be far from campus activities, and you'll find it harder to meet new people.

From a financial standpoint, grants, scholarships, and loans all require that you spend the money on qualified school expenses, which can include room and board. You might not be able to use that money towards rent off-campus. Make sure you check the requirements of your loans and scholarships before making a decision.

Dorms come with a lot of benefits that off-campus housing probably won't. For instance, you'll be nearby a place to do your laundry. The university keeps up the quality of the building. And you'll be in a safer environment because of the security on campus—you'll probably have to show an ID just to get into the building.

Another thing is that you should have already seen the dorms in your campus tour. You know what to expect as far as layout, space, and location. If you wanted to move off-campus though, you'll have to go from apartment to apartment, looking around and making sure it's a place you want to live. This is tough if you're not familiar with the area. Not only will you be unable to really look at the types of apartments available, you may not even know if you're moving into a bad neighborhood.

Finally, if you live on campus and have a seriously horrible problem with your roommate, you can request to be transferred to another room within the dorm or in another building on campus. You won't find that in an apartment. Once you're in, you're stuck there and responsible for rent until the end of the lease.

As you go into your second or third year and have made a good deal of friends, you should look into off-campus housing. Living off-campus will afford you a little more freedom and privacy. You'll hopefully get a parking pass to leave your car on campus, and you might even find that rent is cheaper somewhere else.

If you choose to go with the dorms, get your housing application in as early as possible. Priority is generally given to upperclassmen first, and freshmen get in on a first come first serve basis. The earlier you get in your application, the better chance you have of getting a nicer dorm. Spots fill up quick.

Leave Non-Essentials At Home

If you don't need it, leave it at home. Dorm rooms are small, and you're most likely sharing it with someone else. Your college should give you your roommates contact information in your welcome packet. Contact them to decide what things you'll bring for the common good. They'll get the mini fridge while you get the microwave. They'll get the shower curtain if you'll bring a plunger, etc. This will also help break the ice when you finally meet.

Make a list of your pins, credit cards (if you have any), registration numbers, and serial numbers on valuables like your computer. Leave that list at home with your parents and make a copy to keep somewhere safe. That way, if you lose any information at school, you can get it quickly. If you'd prefer to be hi-tech, make a list and keep it somewhere you can access it. I use a program called Lastpass to keep that information handy.

You can always come up with your own way of doing it, but remember, it has to be accessible to only you or someone you trust. If your computer of phone gets stolen, you don't want the thief to have access to that information either.

Roommates

You may be going to college with your best friend, and you already know that you're going to room with that person. That's great, and I hope it works out, but I knew people in college that roomed with their high school friends, and it never worked out the way they thought.

Two friends of mine are no longer on speaking terms because of the problems they had living with each other. Another two friends keep in casual contact. It all comes back to the fact that you are going to change in college. You're going to learn and grow.

You might find that your friends in college aren't anything like your friends from high school. This doesn't mean that you're fake or anything like that; it just means that you have new interests and new people to share them with.

Also consider that, up until now, you most likely haven't lived with a non-family member. Another person's home and family dynamic is different from yours. You may have stayed with your best friend before and know their family really well, but you were a guest in that home, not a resident. Just because you can be friends with someone during the day doesn't mean that you two are compatible roommates. Maybe you are and maybe you aren't, but if you choose to hang out with people from high school, you'll be sucked back into the same high school drama. A college sophomore gave me that advice when I visited campus, and from what I saw with my other friends, she was right.

On the other hand, if you're worried about rooming with total strangers, remember that they're in the same situation. You probably filled out some personal information on your housing application about whether messy rooms bother you. Colleges tend to do a fair job of matching up people that are compatible (though sometimes it's based on who's available).

Insurance

If you've had insurance up until this point, chances are your parents were paying for it. They may continue to pay for it, but then again maybe not. Either way, it's important for you to be aware of it. The day will come when you need to pay it yourself.

Your college might offer some form of student insurance, and it's a great thing to look into if you're in the market. They can usually offer good rates (because they know you're students) and most likely have a health services building somewhere on campus.

You should talk to your parents about the insurance situation. It may be that your student rates are lower than what your parents pay currently, and they may want to switch. Visit your school website or talk to someone involved with Freshman Orientation to see if there are any health insurance programs available.

While we're on the topic of health, before you go, you should make sure you're up to date on your vaccinations—you're going to be in contact with classes of 100+ people, so your chances of catching something increase. You should also get a physical before you go to make sure everything is okay. Many colleges will require you to do this anyway.

Make a list of allergies to keep handy. Maybe give it to your RA and roommates so that if something does happen, they can give it to the EMTs. If you have any prescriptions, go to your pharmacy and get them transferred to one near your school.

I'm not trying to freak you out. You'll be fine. Expect the best, prepare for the worst.

Selecting Your Major

Unless you're going to a specialized college, you don't even have to think about this now. Even if you had tons of AP credits, you'll still have to take General Education courses, which will keep you busy for the first year at least. Everyone, from English majors to Engineers, has to take these courses, and a lot of them are introductory. Freshman Lit, for example, is required unless you tested out of it.

If you want to go to a tech school for engineering or a performing arts school for dance, then you'll need to know your major before you even pick your college. But then, if this is the path you've chosen, you probably don't need a lot of help figuring out what you want to do after graduation.

On the other hand, you know you want to go to college, but you have no idea what you want to do afterward. That's ok, too. It's easy to change majors, so don't feel like you need to go to school knowing exactly what you're going to do.

You're going to get exposed to so many new things, and you're going to learn about studies and careers you've never even heard of before. It's no wonder so many students change their majors after their first year.

If you know what it is you want to do with your life, then all the power to you. If you're like most of us were, then you'll probably end up changing your major at least once. There's no shame in that, but when you change a major, you want to make sure that you're still going to be able to complete all of your required credits.

Here are a few tips to help you graduate on time.

Read your student book. Colleges don't make a secret of what they expect of you to graduate. They put their requirements in your information packet when you arrive and put it online. Study it, and know it. What classes have you signed up for that will count towards your GenEd?

Make a spreadsheet. At the top of each row, put the requirement, for example Fine Arts, Math/Science, Art/History, whatever it is. Also, put how many classes of each you're required to take.

Next, make columns for your major and minor. Majors and minors will have a few required courses (usually low-level) and then several electives from a certain list. Go through each list and see what's offered at your school. Remember that just because a class is offered at your college, doesn't mean it's offered year-round. Don't wait until the last minute to get all of your classes done.

Start entering in the names of the corresponding classes in the fields below. Make sure to put how many credit hours each one is worth as well. Colleges, in addition to general education and major requirements, want you to have completed a certain number of total credit hours. AP credits can usually count towards them, but not always. You don't want to get to your last semester just to find out you need 2 more credits.

Put more classes than you need. If you took AP classes and the credit transferred, be sure to include the college equivalent in this spreadsheet along with their credit hours.

For every course you complete, highlight it. I used blue for completed classes (don't delete classes when you finish them because it makes it much harder to spot a mistake or miscalculation in later semesters). Sometimes, colleges change their requirements, so it helps to have an accessible past record of what you've done. For every course you are taking currently, highlight it a different color (like green). When courses for next semester get published, highlight them in yellow if you plan to take them. Finally, any courses that have prerequisites, highlight in red until you complete them.

Get your required courses out of the way as soon as possible. Required courses tend to fill up quickly, so jump on them as soon as you can. Electives are less competitive, and if you get to your final semester and the elective you want isn't available, then you can at least choose another elective to graduate on time. Not so with a required course.

For a sample of the worksheet I used, visit my website at http://austinfadely.com/downloads/. Look for the Graduation Planner Sample.

It may seem a little daunting at first, but as you progress through your classes, you'll notice more and more blue on your sheet, and you'll get a sense of accomplishment. Not only that, but you have a convenient reference for the classes you took rather than having to pour through old transcripts. This method will help you keep track of your General Education courses if you decide to switch majors.

By now you should be better prepared for what to expect. This is a time of big, exciting change in your life. With all the moving parts going on, it's easy to get overwhelmed and forget a few things. Don't sweat the small stuff. The next chapter will deal with ways to work smarter, so you can stay focused while remaining calm.

Chapter 8

Efficiency Hacks for Working Smarter

Efficiency is a huge deal in the professional world. Companies fork out mountains of dough every year to consultants that can help increase their working efficiency. There's a lot of literature and theory on how to do things better and more quickly.

There is no better place to learn and use these skills than in college. In this chapter, I'm going to give you tricks and habits that you can develop to work smarter. You'll learn how to focus your energies into tasks that work and give you a better return for your time. Using these same tactics, I improved my grades and spent less time studying than many of my classmates.

A lot of these tips are easy to understand, but it takes discipline and practice to make them habits. Too often, people slip into their old dysfunctional ways and find it hard to change. The critical thing to do is practice what I'm about to tell you.

Some of the models I'll describe were developed for business, but they can apply anywhere: school, personal life, and work.

The first concept I'd like to introduce is something called Getting Things Done or GTD. David Allen came up with the concept, and it's a methodology to help people prioritize their tasks each day. You can start using these strategies now and apply them towards school. Not only will you get better at doing what you do, but you'll also be well practiced by the time you get into your career.

Although many of the techniques make more sense within a company framework, I have adapted them to make sense to the school setting. Here is a list of practices to help you get things done.

Start off each day with 2 or 3 big goals in mind. These are your must-dos. If you make it through the day and all you got done were these goals, then you'd still have had a productive day.

Alternate working and breaks. Don't expect that you're going to sit down and work for a solid four hours. Your mind doesn't work that way. You have to take breaks. When you take these breaks is up to you. I'd recommend breaking up each hour into intervals. Work for a half hour, and then take a break for 5 minutes. Once the 5 minutes are up, start working again—no excuses. You can vary this schedule based on what you're doing and the project you're working on, for example, if you're on a roll, work 50 minutes then take a 10 minute break, but once you pick a workable ratio, stick to it. Don't keep your breaks that long because you'll have a harder time getting back into a working rhythm.

Break up your larger projects. Don't try to write a paper in one day. For one thing, you can't just sit down for four hours and crank out a decent paper with the rest of the night to spare. You might start strong, but maybe an hour into it, you'll wind up staring at the screen or checking Facebook. Four hours is a solid chunk of time to work on one thing, so break up your projects. Here is an example of how to accomplish this for writing research papers:

> Set up one night to research the paper. You have a topic, and you may have an idea of how to approach writing it, but you need sources that support your thesis. Spend two hours at the library finding these sources. College professors like to see that you've thoroughly researched the subject. For instance, some of your sources should be books, while others could be magazines or newspaper articles, and you can always include a few Internet sources. Try to avoid citing nothing but Internet articles though. Once you've got everything you think you'll need for your paper, check out the books, write down the magazine articles, and bookmark the web pages (or email them to yourself). Now you've got the sources you need for your paper.
>
> Over the next few days, read your sources. Take notes as you read. Don't expect that you'll remember where a specific quote is later. Make an outline as you go along, but leave the thesis for last. Keep track of quotes you'd like to use. Write down where to find them and what they support. Once you have enough information, use what you gathered to form your argument and

make a thesis on your outline.

Now that you have the information you need, have read the material, and have a working outline with where to find your quotes, writing the paper won't be nearly as difficult. Now it's time to sit down and write the first draft.

Once your first draft is finished, save and back it up. You can email it to yourself, or you can use a cloud service like dropbox (they have a free version), you can also use flash drives if you have some. I prefer online back-ups because you can access it from any computer, and you can't lose it or damage it like a flash drive. When you finish your first draft, don't work on it for the rest of the day.

After a good night's sleep, start editing your paper. Make sure everything makes sense. Use the same process discussed in Chapter 5. The last thing you should work on is making sure that you used the correct citation format. Proper citation is a big thing in college, which is why you should invest in a style manual for MLA, APA, and CMS. You can usually find one book with all of these styles. If you want, you can take your paper for peer review or the writing center. The point is to separate editing and writing by at least 24 hours—after a night's sleep.

As you can see, there's a significant amount of prep and post work outside of writing the actual paper. Plan it out.

Isolate yourself. Study groups rarely work among friends because you're going to socialize. It's human nature. You need to find a quiet place, away from TVs and friends. Turn off your phone; you're not available during study hours. Now your computer presents a particular problem. Let's say you're working on a research project, you need a computer with an Internet connection to do your research, but you also have access to Facebook, online games, and other time wasters. There are tons of apps to help you block distracting sites. I use StayFocusd, a Chrome browser extension. You can use this app to block sites that you know will tempt you to procrastinate. When you're done, you can unlock those sites until the next study session.

Wake up earlier. This goes back to isolating yourself. College students are notorious night owls, and rest assured your friends will probably want you to go out. It would be great to, and you might try to rush the rest of your study session so you can get to the party. Rather than try to study at night, when your brain is tired anyway, wake up a little earlier every day. Just that extra half hour or so of uninterrupted time will not only help you get more done, but it will set the tone for the rest of the day.

Eat better food. Eat food that will actually give you energy and not rob you of it. High fiber and vitamins are what you're looking for.

For every class, make a list of actionable items at the end of it. For instance, if in your notes, you had a few questions, make sure you list them out at the end of your notes. Write in any assignments or an intention to speak with the professor. This will act as a to-do list.

Complete them before the next class.

Keep a personal, as well as a study calendar. Keep track of all of your committed time. Google lets you create different types of calendars and color code them. Most calendar applications have some method of categorizing your activities. I'd recommend making absolute commitments in red, tentative commitments in yellow, and anything that you can reschedule if you have to can be in green. Make sure to schedule in your trips. It's important to know when you'll be going out of town; it takes time to pack after all. You can also set recurring reminders for yourself to tell you to check your notes for those actionable items from class.

Write down everything you have to do and put them all in one place. If you keep different notebooks for classes, it's a pain to have to keep flipping through 4 or 5 of them just to make a list of things you have to do. Google Calendar is a great place to keep these tasks, since you can set reminders. You'll have to do it for work anyway, so you might as well practice it now.

When you look at your calendar, always look a few weeks ahead. If you only look from week to week, those big projects will sneak up on you. You may not know that you have seven commitments two Fridays from now. If you keep an eye out for what's to come, you'll have time to adjust your schedule to make everything work. On the other hand, if you deal with items as they come along, you'll end up having more than a few sleepless, stress-filled, caffeine-induced nights of work ahead of you.

Like most students, you probably have a couple outside interests, things not related to school. Let's say you want to be a concert violinist, or possibly the next great author. Scheduling tasks for yourself is more difficult because they often get sacrificed and put off. You have to take time to schedule in the things you want to do and pursue as well as the things you have to. Sure, you may have a hectic schedule, and there will probably be a week or two where you can do nothing but what you have to do and rest. But if you don't bother to plan your outside interests, you'll end up not doing them.

The problem with those types of activities is that you don't have anyone to answer to. There's no gun to your head, no deadline to meet, only yourself. See if this scenario sounds familiar: you just finished a grueling exam, one for which you studied all week and didn't get to work on a story you're writing. You go home and have the rest of the day free to work on your story, but as you sit down, your friend texts and asks if you want to hang out. You think to yourself, as you morosely stare at a blank screen, you know, I deserve a little break. You spend the rest of the day with your friend and don't do any work on your story. You wake up the next day guilty that you didn't get anything done.

You can replace writing a story with just about anything. The problem isn't that you're not disciplined enough: it's just that you don't have a clearly defined goal. You know you won't finish your story in one sitting, but you neglect to break up the work into definable parts. When you don't have a clear goal, it's hard to see the progress you've made. That makes you less apt to work because the reward isn't visible enough. Large projects take patience, but the modern brain is getting conditioned more and more for instant gratification. The model goes a little something like this: task-reward, task-reward. School is set up to constantly reward good work with grades. How many projects do you have in a single class? And how quickly do you get your grade when you finish an assignment? A week or two at the most, right?

Larger projects like writing a story or a book take a lot more patience since the reward is so far off. It's like running a marathon. If you start the race thinking about the 26 miles, you'll get disheartened. You start breathing a little more heavily and your legs get a little uncomfortable. How can you last for 23 more miles? Running, like most sports, is a constant mental battle. Sure, you need to be in shape—that definitely helps, but nobody breezes through a marathon. The point is that physical conditioning can only get you so far, but the ones that triumph have that mental toughness to keep driving them on. Here's the thing about that though: being mentally tough doesn't mean you see the end goal and simply will it hard enough into existence; you break down the end goal into attainable chunks. Marathon runners don't run 26 miles: they run 1 mile 26 times.

Setting Goals

When you break up your large goals into manageable parts, you create a task-reward system that keeps you engaged with what you're doing.

So going back to your short story, the problem wasn't so much that you weren't disciplined: it's just that you didn't have an immediately recognizable goal. You simply wanted to work on your story, which though it seems straightforward, is actually vague. How long do you want to work on your story for? One hour, two hours? Do you want to write 500 words, 1,000? If instead, you knew these answers beforehand, you would have had a specific goal, had a better understanding of the time it would take to achieve that goal, and would have been less tempted to shirk it altogether.

Most of the time, we keep goals too general or grandiose, meaning they aren't specific enough for us to realize when we've accomplished them, or they or too large for us to actively work on them. So when setting your goals, remember to break them down and make them specific. You can do this any way that works for you, or you can make them SMART.

S is for Specific.

Make your goals specific enough so that you know what they are. Studying Algebra isn't specific. I would rather say, I will learn to multiply binomials.

M is for Measurable.

How do you know when you've achieved your goal? If you can't answer the question, then your goal isn't measurable. You need clear success criteria.

A is for Attainable.

Don't make impossible goals. This isn't the same as making improbable goals because with enough drive and work, you can accomplish most anything. But keep it within the realm of possibility. For instance, saying you'll figure out how to fly using nothing but some kerosene, a skateboard and a crap load of pillowcases is not an attainable goal.

R is for Realistic

Although progress feels great, nothing can be more frustrating than stagnation. You don't want to feel you've run into a wall because it's a constant struggle at that point. If it's not realistic, there's no point in having a goal. You already have enough obstacles to overcome, don't make an unrealistic goal one of them. Getting an A on an exam by tomorrow when you haven't studied all semester is not realistic.

T is for Time-bound

Put a limit on it. That's the whole point of a deadline. If you don't set a deadline, that little voice that says you can put it off another day will have little to contend against it.

Now you have SMART goals, where you can limit the amount of work it takes to accomplish each one, and you have also set up your rewards along the way. When you apply SMART to a big project, make a list of each smaller item. As you go through them, cross off each one throughout the project. Don't focus on how many tasks you have left, instead focus only on the next one. As you get further along, you'll notice your list getting smaller with more crossed out lines than tasks left. There's no better feeling than a sense of accomplishment.

Creating Accountability

Accountability is huge. You need someone to be accountable to for every single one of your goals; someone who will keep you focused and drive you to work harder. Accountability is meeting deadlines.

Most of the time, teachers, coaches, bosses, and parents impose deadlines on us. We don't have to worry about deciding when the deadline will be because it's given to us, but that won't always be the case.

In school, you might have a deadline given to you for an assignment, but remember what we said about keeping your goals SMART? Writing a paper is not specific, and saying you'll finish by the deadline isn't truly time-bound. For something like a paper, you have to break down the project into smaller pieces and create the deadlines for those pieces yourself.

Once you've set your deadlines, get someone to be your accountability partner. It can be your parents or a classmate. Once you involve someone else, you've made your deadlines public. You'll be more driven to meet your deadlines because you're expected to do so. If nobody knows about your deadlines, nobody is going to ask you about it or get you on track.

Prioritizing Tasks

In college, not everything will get done. You will need to learn to prioritize. When your demands are few, you can generally follow a chronological format, meaning you do things in the order in which they're due. This may have worked just fine for you in the past. In college, however, and definitely in the professional world, you'll find that different tasks demand your time simultaneously.

Multitasking is a complete lie—there is no such thing. Your brain has a mindshare value, let's say 10. When you're doing homework, you should be completely focused, meaning you're using all 10 of your mindshare value on homework. If you turn on the music, then it becomes more like 8 on homework and 2 on music. Add in the TV, and it's like 5 on TV and 5 on homework. The point is, at the end of that half hour, you either don't really know what was happening in the show, or you got very little done on your homework…most of the time it's both. You can't research a history paper and carry on 4 IM conversations effectively, so don't bother.

In any case, when you come across a situation where you have to do two things and only have time to do one, remember that you won't be able to multitask to increase your efficiency. Instead, you have to learn to prioritize. Choose the one that will give you the greatest benefit.

There is no one right framework to use. I've read about and experimented with several ways to prioritize. Though I haven't found one approach that works for everything, I've found a few that are useful in different situations, and here's what they are:

CARVER

CARVER is an acronym for Critical, Accessible, Return, Vulnerability, Effect, and Recognizability. I first encountered it as a project manager for a design agency. It proved useful when deciding how to allocate scarce resources for internal projects. It's equally useful for prioritizing major personal projects.

Critical – How critical is this task? What will it accomplish? This is pretty straightforward. The greater the consequence (payoff) the more critical it is.

Accessible – How accessible are the resources required to accomplish this task? You may find for example that you're working on a group project, and you can't start your portion until your partner delivers hers. This example shows low accessibility.

Return – What sort of return can you expect? Is the project worth 5% of your grade or 20% of your grade? A high score on a more heavily weighted project has a higher return.

Vulnerability – How easily can the task be achieved? Can you knock it out in a few hours or will it take a while to do? The less effort it takes, the greater the vulnerability.

Effect – What effect will achieving your goal have? A high score in an elective is great, but compared to a high score on a core class; it's not as good. An example might be, if I get a great score on this report for English, I'll pull my grade up enough to get an A, which will look better than an A in pottery.

Recognizability – How well can you articulate the reason for the task? This is especially important on college applications. If you spent a lot of time working on a project, you need to be able to articulate why it was important. Here's an example: Marris spent 3 hours after school each day volunteering at the Marine Science Center down the road. She ended up working on a project that led to better water quality in the surrounding area. This task is easy to articulate; therefore, it has a high recognizability score.

Pareto's Law

Pareto's Law is better known as the 80/20 rule. You get 80% of your return from 20% of your effort. The other 80% of your time is wasted getting only 20% of the return. I recently read a book by Richard Koch called *The 80/20 Manager*. Koch argues that we should identify the 20% of what we do that brings us 80% of the return, and focus solely on those tasks. I've developed a scoring sheet to help classify tasks in just that way. It's great for getting the most for your effort, but it ignores magnitude of return. Basically, a medium return task with low effort will be a better choice than a high return task that has a high level of effort in this approach. The purpose, of course, is to find those 80/20 opportunities, not necessarily the greatest return.

7-Habits

Stephen Covey wrote *The 7 Habits of Highly Effective People*. Among other things, Covey discusses the need for people to prioritize everything in their lives, not just what they see in the workplace. Everything is either urgent or not urgent, and important or not important. Covey argues that we get bogged down in the urgent and unimportant category, when we should be striving to get to the not urgent but important tasks. Because this is a categorical strategy, it's simpler to use. The only drawback is that two tasks in the same category won't have any way to outweigh one another.

I've put together a prioritization calculator in Excel. Use it the next time you have some choices to make in terms of how you spend your time. I recommend including all tasks in here, not just work related ones. The ultimate goal is to bring more value to our lives, not just our companies.

You can download the prioritization calculator at my website: http://austinfadely.com/downloads/.

Organizing

Being organized goes a long way in cutting the amount of time it takes to do something. The biggest obstacle is creating a methodology and sticking to it. It takes discipline to stay organized, and it's a constant battle. The reward, however, is often great, so it pays to make the big initial effort of devising a system and training yourself to stick to it. Once you make it a habit, you'll find it will come quite naturally.

First things first, get a file crate—they cost all but $3, and they allow you to keep all of your relevant files in one place. Then get a pack of hanging folders with labels. Use those labels! Make sure you have an easy-to-identify system so that if you have to tell your parents where something is, they can locate it easily. Each system is prone to different needs, but here are a few ideas for folder categories:

College Applications

App. Requirements—School 1

App. Requirements—School 2, etc.

Letters of Recommendation (You'll want to keep these in case you can use them for multiple applications)

Personal Essays (maybe a good place to store ideas for admissions essays)

Work samples (especially for art/photography majors)

SAT/ACT Test Scores (Keep your copies!)

Medical information (Every school needs to know you're up on your vaccinations. it's easier to have them rather than hunt them down later. You might also have a copy of your birth certificate here.)

I'm sure you can think of several more; these are just a few ideas to help get you started.

You can use it for school, but it's not a handy place to keep important tasks. The reason is that it's easy to forget something you shove in a crate. Use an online calendar or some other method for reminders about deadlines. Remember that it must be part of your routine to check it so that you won't forget anything. That is the whole point.

Think of the crate as a reference library. Keep college applications, essays about yourself, and school information in it. You might also see if your parents have a handy system for getting at their recent year's tax returns because you'll need them to fill out the FAFSA. If they don't, see if they'll let you get copies to keep in your crate. There's nothing worse than discovering you can't complete an application because you've misplaced some vital information.

Once you have a good system in place, you'll find that locating all the needed documents for anything becomes a simple task.

Are you ready for the challenge?

The college atmosphere is completely different from high school. Although AP classes can help prepare you for a more difficult curriculum, you won't be exposed to a completely college-style classroom. Also consider that many AP classes are the same as one college course, so you spend 9 months learning in high school what you would learn in 4 months in college.

College classrooms are set-up differently, and class sizes are different. Your first few classes will probably be in large lecture halls with a couple hundred other students. Freshmen intro classes are a lot like that. Once you start to specialize and take higher levels towards your major, your classes will have fewer and fewer students.

In a class of 300, you can't expect to get much help from the professor; in fact, more than likely you'll be assigned a Teaching Assistant (usually a grad student) with fifty other students. It is imperative that you can teach yourself from a book. You should also get to know some of your classmates and organize study sessions.

You may not feel like you should have to take Biology if you're going to major in Fine Arts, but that's just the way of the world. Accept that you'll be responsible to meet your General Education Requirements, and be ready to spend more time studying for your weaker areas.

Another thing about learning in a large lecture hall is that the teaching is simply not as interactive as when there are twelve students. The professor cannot divide his time getting everyone involved. However, most institutions are getting a more high tech infrastructure. For example, you might be required to buy an electronic remote, so periodically the professor can poll the class with a random question.

College classrooms also have a lot more freedom in their structure and content. The University itself confers your degree, unlike public high school, where you get your diploma from the County or Municipal Board of Education. The University has more flexibility to determine the requirements for a degree. In high school, you prepare for a county, city, or statewide test. AP courses prepare you for a national test. In college, however, the professor usually writes the exams, and sometimes the textbooks as well. Because of that, any practice exams you find will have to be on your own time. There won't be extra projects, and there won't be worksheets. You might take a class where you have only two grades: the midterm and a final. Other classes are based heavily on essays. When you have three opportunities in a class to get a grade, each one counts much more than they did in high school, so you have to prepare well.

Larger classrooms are taught lecture style, meaning the professor will tell you what you need to know, and you'll have to take notes quickly. Hopefully, the professor prepares PowerPoint presentations that you can download online to help with your notes, but nothing can replace your own notes. The reason is that you think the way you think, and the notes you take aren't meant to replace what you hear in class; they're supposed to help you remember what you learned. Your notes are most effective for you because your memory is subject to the quirks of your learning style. For example, you may perfectly understand the names and functions of different neurotransmitters in the brain, so your notes will be less extensive in this area than someone that doesn't. Remember, you're keeping up with a lecture, so develop a shorthand and fill in the details later while it's still fresh in your head. Don't rely on yourself to remember too much; it will bite you in the behind later in the semester.

In college, you'll learn to develop a lot of tricks. You'll learn, for instance, that the best place to study has the least distractions, which usually means the library. Notes are most effective when you read them. One tactic I used was to take notes in class on a notebook. I had one notebook for all of my classes, but at the end of the week, I would enter those notes into my computer. This did two things: it gave me one more point of contact with the material I was supposed to learn, and it allowed me to organize my notes while the lectures were still fresh in my mind. I could elaborate on my shorthand and arrange my notes so they were easier to read and understand. That way, by exam time, I had heard the lecture, written notes, and copied them into the computer. At the end of it, I had been exposed 3 times to the material, and I had notes I could read and understand.

I also like the notebook approach because it keeps your writing muscles strong. Typing uses different muscles, and if you don't write a lot, you'll get hand cramps during essay-style exams.

If you're slow at note taking, you can practice by taking notes on your favorite shows. Write the action, what happens, who does what, and develop a shorthand. Make sure you've seen the episode before. When you're done, re-read your notes, and see if you missed anything.

Once you've got that down, try it with a movie you've never seen before.

Use cues from the movie to let you know important plot points. You'll be able to apply this talent in the classroom as you notice your professor's cues. You'll eventually learn that getting a good grade isn't as much about reading the book as it is about reading the professor. They already know what's on the exam and what they're going to test you on. You'll start to figure out what sounds like something important and what doesn't.

I had a psychology professor that loved to use students as hypothetical examples.

> So Sam here is serotonin. He's trying to make it to Emilio, the next nerve receptor. The problem is that once Sam makes it to Emilio, he comes back to his neuron too quickly and repeats the process. Sam is doing it so much that it's throwing our patient's brain chemistry out of whack. So we prescribe an SSRI, so Gloria here, is going to block Sam from getting back to his neuron. Our patient's serotonin levels decrease, and she feels happier.

Obviously, I don't need to know who Sam, Gloria, or Emilio are for the test, but I'd probably need to know what an SSRI does. If the professor's story works for you, copy it down. If not, put it in your own words.

Another great trick is, ready for it: reading. Yes, I'm plugging it again because I cannot stress enough how much reading will help you prepare for college. Like everything else, it takes practice. You can pick up speed, read more quickly, and expand your vocabulary all at once. Trust me, when you have to read chapters of text before your next class, you'll be happy you took the time in high school to sharpen your reading skills.

Chapter 9

Personal and Financial Management

Everyone needs to know how to manage their time and finances. These skills are critical, yet they are rarely taught in schools. Most people I know had to learn these things the hard way, and I did too. I had my share of missed appointments, and mismanaging finances got me into some unhealthy credit card debt.

The big irony is that personal and financial management isn't difficult to understand: it's just not something people teach you. In this chapter, I'm going to pass on some of the life-saving tips I picked up along the way. You'll learn basic time management, how to create a budget (very important for college students), and how to build credit so that you can one day buy a car or a house. Trust me, learning this stuff early can easily save you countless headaches, not to mention thousands of dollars in the long haul.

Managing Your Time

The reason many colleges like to see extra-curricular activities on your application is because they need to know if you can manage your time wisely. The key to successful time management is by keeping a daily planner. Either in print or electronically, keeping a schedule is a great practice to get into. Google has a free calendar application that sends you reminders of upcoming events. You can also use iCal if you're an Apple user. Get in the habit of doing it sooner rather than later. Like all good practices, it takes time to make it a habit.

Setting up a Google Calendar is pretty simple. First, you'll have to create a Google account. This is a good opportunity to create a professional looking email address if you haven't yet.

Once you've set up your account, go to calendar.

You can choose different views for day, week, and month. To add an event, all you have to do is click on the right time slot and start typing information in. Once you've created the event, you can edit details by double clicking on it. From there, you can set reminders for yourself, recurrences if it happens daily or weekly, and you can invite others by sending it to their email addresses. This is great for organizing study hours.

You can also create different calendars for different purposes; for instance, you may keep a personal calendar that's private; then you might have a shared calendar with your roommates to let them know when you'll be around.

Get into the habit of using some sort of scheduling tool now because it will be a lot easier when you have to use one for work. A few companies I've worked with use Google Apps for Business, and many companies use Microsoft Outlook. I'd highly recommend being familiar with at least one if not both of these platforms.

You can sync your calendar with your phone, too. Even feature phones have calendars in them. Granted, it's a pain to enter all of your information at first, but set aside some time to set it up. Having a reminder on the go is an invaluable tool you shouldn't pass up.

Schedule planning is even more important when others are involved. If you're working on a group project, it's just common courtesy to let everyone know when you expect to be done with your portion. This has two benefits: it forces you to be accountable, and it's a great habit to have once you start working. Your future boss will need status reports, and if you're already in the habit of giving them, then you're much better off.

Remember that calendars only work if you're disciplined about entering information into them. You can spend some time setting up a schedule, but if you never revisit it, it loses its value.

Another thing you need to start doing is eliminating distractions. Studying in front of the TV is not a good practice. Some people even have a hard time studying at home because there are so many things to distract them. College will be more of a challenge. Now there are roommates to distract you. Even if you plan on studying all night, some noisy neighbors may be throwing a small party. Changing your surroundings can make all the difference in the world.

The library is often a great place to study because it is quiet, and there is little else to do other than read. You may find that two hours spent studying there is the same as four or six hours in your dorm. Knowing where your time is best spent is part of good personal management. Keeping a schedule will help you avoid procrastinating and make for much less stressful times before exams.

I said it before, but it's important: set goals for yourself and stick to them. One of the hardest disciplines is self-discipline. Give yourself manageable deadlines and stick to them. Focus on results and not on input. For example, don't study with the mindset that you will do it for 2 hours and then stop. Hours studied is an input for a result. Good grades come from results. Instead, let's say you want to understand differential equations. Study with the intent to master something you have trouble with or review something you're hazy on. Don't worry so much about how much time you spend. Care about the outcome. The outcome, e.g.:

mastering differential equations, is what will help you ace an exam.

Don't wait until you're in college to put these tips to use. Habits take time to acquire, so start sooner rather than later. You'll find that if you make these skills a priority, the college admissions process will become much easier. Deadlines won't sneak up on you, and you'll have ample time to get your applications finished and proofread before sending them in.

Building Wealth

Building wealth starts early. The younger you are when you understand how to save and invest money, the more potential you have to make. You may already have a job or an allowance, and perhaps you know the difference between a checking and a savings account. Even so, you should take some time to learn about different ways to manage your money, so that you have an easier time once you graduate.

The first thing you should do, if you haven't already, is get a checking and a savings account.

There are usually banks on or near campus, but you don't have to use them. You can open up accounts at multiple banks in fact. If you can, look into a credit union. They tend to offer better rates than banks, but they are very local, so they won't have a lot of ATMs if you travel outside the area.

When you get your checking account, you'll have to buy checks, and you'll be issued a check/debit card. To use the card, you'll need to create a secret PIN. The nice thing about check cards is that you can use them as debit, which means your bank deducts the money from your account immediately, or you can use them as credit. Credit transactions take a few days to post to your account.

Your checkbook will come with a transaction register, which is where you'll record everything you deposit and withdraw. Whatever you do with this account—get money from the ATM, make automatic deposits, pay with checks, or spend with your debit card—you need to keep record of it in your register. Seems obvious right? Still, some people forget to do it.

You'll want to balance your checkbook at least once a month. Because I often lived so close to a 0 balance in college, I had to do it more often. All you have to do is compare your bank statement to your register. If everything matches, you're good to go. If there is a discrepancy, you'll have to go back over your transactions and see if you missed anything. If you keep good records, this won't be a big hassle.

I cannot stress how important it is to be up to date with your account. It's when you lose track that you fall behind, miss payments, and bounce checks.

Now you have an account where you can deposit your money, but what is the savings account for?

You should set a goal of saving 5% of your income per month. Set aside that money, and put it into your savings. Do not touch it. Slowly, it will build up to say one or two thousand dollars. Ideally, you'll keep building it up to cover a couple month's worth of expenses. You now have a cushion and a little bit of relief for those post-college years.

Once you have enough in savings to cover you for a few months, start investing in higher return instruments like Money Market Accounts or an IRA. By saving so early, you let compound interest work for you and make you exponentially more money.

Controlling Costs

Budgets aren't just for people with little money. Every Fortune 500 Company has a budget because it's not about limiting spending as it is about tracking it. Knowing where your money goes each month will work to your favor no matter how much or how little money you have.

Mint.com has a fantastic site (and mobile app) where you input all of your accounts, and it keeps track of your spending for you. Each month, you can view trends in your spending to see where your money is going. It even has a way for you to record cash exchanges. It's important to remember to keep track of your cash spending. This is particularly important if you have a job where you collect cash tips. Don't keep all of the money you make in your wallet. Set some aside or deposit it. If you don't have access to it, you'll be less likely to spend it.

Intuit owns mint.com. They're the same people that do QuickBooks and TurboTax. Their site is completely safe, but if you're squeamish about putting that kind of information in one place online, you can always create a spreadsheet to track it. The only thing is remembering to hang on to all of your receipts and entering them in manually. Checking your budget on a weekly basis will help you make sure that you aren't spending more than you're making.

If you decide to create your budget on a spreadsheet, here is a step-by-step way to do it:

1. Use one page for each month. This will allow you to scan back through previous months quickly and easily.

2. Divide your spending into categories. Some examples include: rent, loans, groceries, dining out, cleaning supplies, entertainment, power, cable, gas, gifts, clothes, automobile, insurance, cell phone, miscellaneous necessities (like haircuts).

3. Categorize each expenditure into one of these several categories. You can use the sum feature in Excel to find out exactly how much you spend on dining out each month. Categories like rent and loan payments are constant, but it's helpful to know how much money you need to get by. You'll also be able to see how much more money you'll need for seasonal items (you can make up a category and use it for one or two months. For example Christmas gifts, or taxes).

4. Keep track of your income against your expenses. This is also helpful if you work for tips or don't get a steady paycheck. You'll

be able to see when you make the most money and how much you can count on getting each month.

5. After a specific period, whether six months or a year, find the total amount of expenses per category. This will give you an idea of how much you need to make annually.

6. Make charts for each month. Pie charts work well for expenses by category. Double bar graphs work well for comparing expenses versus income.

7. Now you have a workable budget! Take advantage of it. Review it, and see where you can cut back if you have to. You'll know exactly how much extra money you make each month and will be less likely to spend too much.

Here are some examples of the kind of tracking you should be doing with your budget.

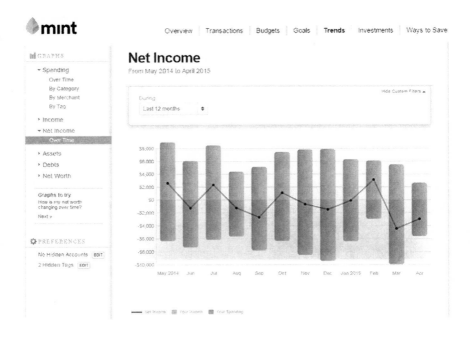

Net Income over time tells you your overall cash flow over time. You want a positive average each month, which means you're making more than you're spending.

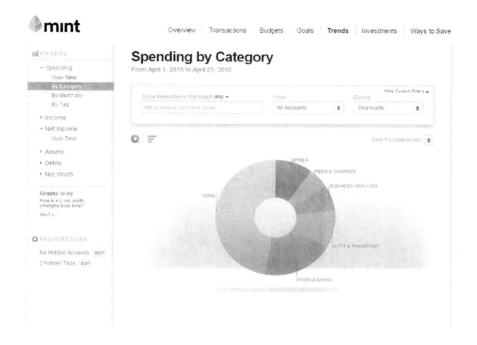

Spending by Category tells you where your money goes. You should expect to see a fairly constant breakdown, but some months will be different (like during the holidays or tax season).

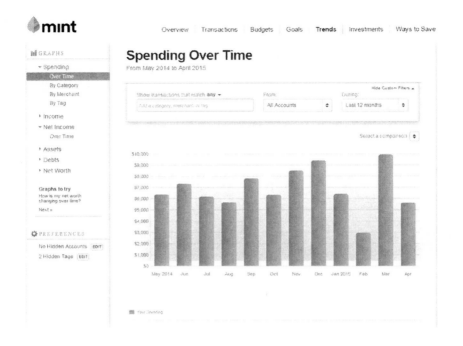

Spending Over Time tells you which months are your most expensive. See the big spike in April? That was tax season.

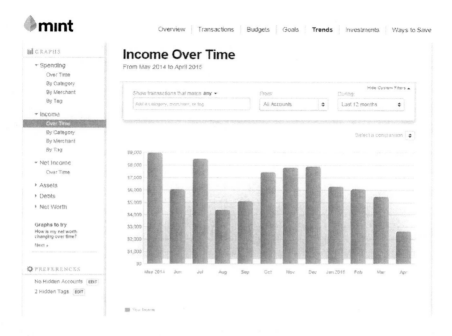

Income Over Time is really only helpful if you have variable income. People that work for tips and freelancers will find this type of information helpful. Salaried employees know what they make each month.

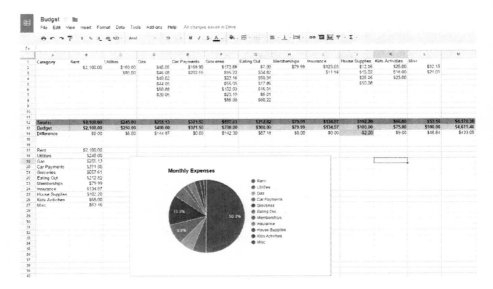

You can recreate many of the same reports using Excel or Google Sheets. Here is an example of Spending by Category from a spreadsheet I used to track finances before I found out about Mint.

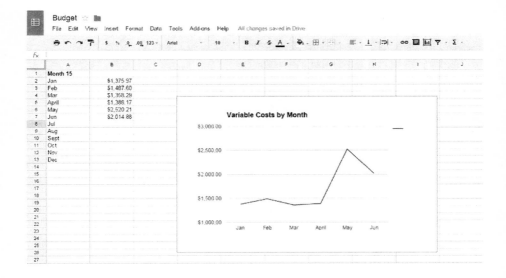

Spreadsheets give you more flexibility in terms of how you analyze your money. Variable Costs by Month lets you track flexible spending categories—things like groceries, gas, restaurants, and misc. By removing fixed costs like rent, you can focus more on where you can save money.

It's up to you how many categories you have, but you should always budget for fun money. Dave Ramsey calls it a blow category, and it's simply that—money you intend to have fun with. If you don't account for it, you'll do it anyway and won't be able to stay under budget.

I know what you're thinking. This all seems so easy, and it is! The difficult part is not understanding: it's practice. You have to keep being disciplined about it. Just like a calendar, you can spend a lot of time writing up a budget, but it won't work if you don't keep at it.

You'll probably find that you go over budget consistently as you start out. You can either adjust your budget or adjust your spending behavior. As you continue the practice, you'll hone your budget.

This practice will help you understand the real cost of living, so when you do get a job after college, you'll know if your pay will sustain your lifestyle. You'll also be able to grasp how your student loan bills will affect your total monthly spending.

Now that you've got the basics of saving and budgeting, let's talk about a typical pitfall for college students—credit cards.

Building Credit

Credit is a tricky thing; it requires discipline to manage it well. It's incredibly easy to get into debt, and not so easy to get out of it. You will need to establish some sort of credit history if you want to buy a house or a car without paying all cash. The first step to avoiding taking on too much debt is to understand it.

There are two major types of debt you can get into. One is installment. These are loans that you pay down on a principal amount. The other is revolving. Revolving debt refers to credit cards, where the balance fluctuates because you can keep putting purchases on the card and pay a portion each month.

Both of these debt types will go into your credit report. Your credit report is used to establish a pattern of your credit history. Companies want to know if you pay on time and if you live within your means.

Having good credit has a lot of benefits. For one, you get access to lower interest rates. The amounts you can borrow are usually higher, and sometimes you won't have to pay deposits when you sign up to cell phone and utility services. Otherwise, some companies will make you pay a deposit on sign-up if you have bad credit.

I assume you already have student loans. That's a type of installment debt. That will go on your credit report, but that alone won't establish a good history. For one thing, you won't need to make any payments until after graduation. Many college students get credit cards. Do so, but be cautious. Before you apply to anything, you need to understand what will help you build good credit.

The main factors considered in your credit report are:

High Impact:

> Credit Card Utilization – this is the percentage of your card limits you are using. You want to be around 30%. If it's much lower than that, then companies assessing your history won't be as certain about your ability to manage debt. You simply haven't taken on enough. If your utilization is too high, it means your monthly payments are high, and companies will know that you may not be able to afford their services.

> Payment History – make your minimum payments on time. If you can meet your obligations, you'll be less of a risk. If you know you'll be late on a payment one month, call the company and work it out. Not every late bill gets reported to a credit agency.

> Derogatory Marks – if you have had accounts go into collection (for lack of payment), this will show up as a derogatory mark. The more you have, the poorer your credit.

Medium Impact:

Age of Credit History – this is the average length of time you've had all of your credit cards. So getting a card or two early can help go a long way by the time you graduate. Every time you get a new card this number will go down.

Low Impact:

Total Number of Accounts – the more diversified your account types are, the better. In addition to major credit cards, you might also consider a gas card and a retail card. You can apply for those at gas stations like Shell or ExxonMobil and at stores like Best Buy or Mattress Firm. These cards won't have a Visa or MasterCard logo on them. They can only be used inside those stores.

Credit Inquiries – every time you apply for a loan or a card, every time you apply for a service for a cell phone or power and electric, every time you apply to rent an apartment or house, you'll get a credit inquiry. Too many inquiries at once can hurt your score a little. It might show that you're trying to apply to too many credit cards, but after 12 months, the inquiries drop off.

Your credit is assessed by three main agencies: Equifax, Experian, and TransUnion. I'd recommend finding a service that lets you review your credit reports from each of these agencies because you don't know which one will get queried in your next application. You might also find discrepancies on them. For example, I had a bad mark on my report because of one of my parent's cards. I was an authorized signatory, but that's not the same as owning the credit card. I disputed the mark and got it removed. My credit score went up.

A little side note: if your parents give you a card that's attached to their account, that won't build your history. It may have your name on it, but it's not your card or your credit.

So now we've pretty much established what good credit history is. You might be ready to apply for cards now, but I want to pass on a few tips so that you don't wind up building up huge amounts of credit card debt like I've seen so many do.

For your first card, get one with a low limit. You'll have less room to get into trouble. My first card had a $1,000 limit, and that was more than enough. You'll have a higher interest rate because you have no established history. Again, join a credit union if you can and get a card there. Credit unions aren't the same as for-profit banks, and their rates tend to be a bit lower. Remember, even if you do qualify for a higher limit, keep the limit low. It will be easier to hit that 30% utilization rate.

Don't get a gas or retail card right away. They have the highest interest rates of any around. They're useful if you use them and pay them off each month. I would avoid carrying a balance on them for utilization because you'll spend more on interest each month.

As a student, you're a target for credit card companies. That's because these companies expect you to put more on the card than you can pay each month; then they get to charge you interest. In my experience, even the best budgeters have bigger balances from time to time. You simply cannot account for all of life's emergencies. Be smart and choose your card wisely. Some have perks and rewards, while others offer lower interest rates, called APR. Some cards have annual fees (American Express typically does). Pay attention to the fine print and pick something that makes sense for you.

Mint.com has a service where it will compare several cards for you and show which ones will save you the most money. A lot of cards will advertise with something like "low rates starting at ..." Just because those cards are available at low rates doesn't mean you'll get them at that rate. Once you apply, the credit card company will check your history and give you an interest rate and limit based on that. Don't always listen to what the advertisement says. Also, be wary of introductory rates. It's very easy to max out a card with 0% APR only to be hit with big interest payments after the introductory period is over.

You can use these other sites to compare credit cards.

http://www.creditcards.com/college-students.php

http://www.cardhub.com

http://www.cardratings.com/studentcreditcards.html

Once you've got your card, use it sparingly. You could put most of your purchases on a debit card, so you can't spend more than you have. But the best approach for keeping your spending in check is to use cash.

From a mental standpoint, you "feel" cash more than credit cards. When you pay in cash, for that brief moment when you look at and hold it, you feel a connection to it. You must physically break the connection between your hand and your money before you can purchase anything. Conversely, credit cards never leave your possession, or, if they do, you get them right back. You haven't physically lost anything. It's a subtle mental cue that allows you to spend more on a card then in cash.

Furthermore, large bills are hard to break. For the same reason you feel cash more than a credit card, it is harder to break a hundred dollar bill than it is a twenty. Your mind may take an extra second to evaluate a purchase, and I'll give you an example. Say you're filling up the tank, and you think you might go inside and get some coffee. Think about how easy it would be to exchange that ten or five dollar bill. Then think about how difficult it would be to exchange a hundred dollar bill for the same drink. Chances are you'll do without the coffee.

The key to good credit is staying in control. Don't let your spending control you, and don't live beyond your means.

Chapter 10

Getting Real World Experience

The number one reason most students go to college is to get a good job. Hopefully by the time you graduate, you will have expanded your circle of friends, increased your understanding, and furthered your knowledge, but a degree doesn't promise anything in terms of a job.

You've probably already heard how important it is to get real-world experience, either through jobs or internships. You don't want to graduate without having done anything outside of school. Companies want to hire people with "experience."

In this chapter, we'll look at the different ways to find good jobs and internships that fit in with what you want to do. The last chapter should have helped you learn how to plan your time, so now we're going to look at some key activities you should be filling your time with.

When you start going out to interviews and meeting potential employers, most if not all will ask you to tell a story where you overcame a hardship. You want something more to talk about than your printer breaking down minutes before a paper is due or how hard your exams were.

When you answer that question, you want to draw on something relevant. Work experience will expose you to people older than you are, and you'll have to learn to get along with a range of personality types. You'll quickly find out that bosses don't have time to hold your hand and walk you through your job step by step. You'll need to think on your feet and solve problems on your own. These are the sorts of relevant skills you need no matter what you do.

Hopefully, you'll have a job lined up once you finish college. If you majored in Engineering, it might be a bit easier for you, especially if you go to your school's career fairs. Many of my friends that were hired before they graduated were engineers. If you're a Liberal Arts major on the other hand, I can tell you your journey is probably going to have a few more turns in it before you land that exciting career.

In any case, you have to start getting experience before you're out in the real world. Get a part-time job or an internship at a major firm. Work hard and get noticed, and you might just get that entry-level position once you graduate. Your chances are much higher if you've got some knowledge and OJT (on-the-job training).

There are two basic forms of "work" for college students. There are internships, and there are jobs. Internships pay you in experience. They're usually better in terms of getting you the kind of experience in the field you want. Jobs tend to have better pay (but that's not always the case).

Jobs

As a college student, you'll find there are typical jobs most students take. Usually they fall in the service industry. I worked as a server and bartender for a while. It was a good experience. Many other students I knew worked in retail.

College is a great time to go out and get a job. If you get into something you don't like, it's much easier to walk away. Bosses that employ college students usually understand that you may be going home over the summer or that you'll need to take off during exam week. They also know students tend to have high turnover. You're also still at that stage in life where it's okay to ask for money to get by for a month or so. Student loans and some scholarships will cover your living expenses while at school. It's a relatively safe environment, so you have the opportunity to walk away from jobs you don't like, at least it's easier than if other people are depending on you to bring home a check.

College is a time where you learn a lot about yourself and the world. Don't write off low paying jobs as something beneath you. The truth is that the best friends you make tend to be the ones that go through hard times with you. There's a sort of camaraderie between people working the same low-paying job. And if you're observant and thoughtful enough, absolutely anything can teach you something.

I spent a lot of time bouncing around jobs in college. My freshman year, I worked as the Data Systems Creator for the Facilities Management plant at my university. I showed up my first day, and my boss walks me into a room with file cabinets, boxes, and binders everywhere. He turns to me and says, "We need to know what's in this room."

For the next three months, I poured over proposals, transcripts, submittals, and blueprints. I didn't have any clue what some of this stuff was, and I was expected to categorize it! Not only that, I had to document it in an electronic database. Was I really going to be able to do this?

Well, two and a half months into it, my system was tested. Someone in the office asked for a specific document. Previously someone would have had to go rifling through the old boxes and file cabinets to find what they were looking for. I checked my spreadsheet, found the cabinet number, and within two minutes had the binder in hand. I was grinning from ear to ear with the satisfaction of a job well done.

The next year, the Facilities Management office did not have the funds to keep me on staff, but I learned something important at the job. Aside from learning about submittals, proposals, and other office stuff, I learned that I could learn a job. It didn't matter how little I understood at first—if I tried enough and spent enough time, I could learn to do the job well. The same is true of anyone willing to apply themselves. You can't buy that kind of satisfaction or confidence.

Never write something off as temporary. You never know what will come of a summer job. I had started working for a publishing company in Baltimore. I was a math checker. I started by doing "cold solves" for math problems in textbooks. After a little time, I got selected to write my own math problems. After that, I had more editing responsibilities. What started out as a single-semester paid internship turned into 8 years of freelance work. It got me through college, graduation, and the Great Recession. I never would have thought that's the type of work I would do, but it turned out to be a lifesaver.

Like I said, don't be afraid to try out different jobs. In college I had a grand total of 6 jobs (not counting working for my father). In addition to the two I mentioned above, I was a server in three different restaurants and a Boy Scout leader for the PAL system in Baltimore County. All of these were part time or seasonal, but I learned a lot about myself in each one. For example, as a server, I learned how to deal with difficult customers and work with people under stress. As a Boy Scout leader, I learned how to teach others and interact with kids.

Different jobs will teach you different skills, but to me, there are really only 3 things you need to get from a job:

> The confidence to know you can learn to do anything well given time

> The patience and tact to deal with difficult people

The people skills to work with others under stress and achieve results

Being successful at any job will require that skill set, and you can learn them in even the unlikeliest of jobs.

Internships

Internships come in different varieties. There are internships that pay you hourly, some pay stipends (a fixed payment), and others pay nothing at all. It really depends on the kind of internship you get that will determine if you'll get paid. Usually, internships in business and journalism are unpaid, but not all of them.

You might think that an unpaid internship is just giving your time away for free. Many students have to work in college, and taking on an internship on top of a job is often too much to balance with schoolwork. You'll have to make the tough decision on whether or not an unpaid internship is right for you. Don't be put off though. College can be busy no question, but most of all, it should be fun and memorable. You ought to be able to look back with a sense of accomplishment and fulfillment. You'll make some of your best friends, and you might even meet your future spouse. You'll broaden your horizons, meet people you thought could exist only on TV, and eat the unhealthiest food of your life.

Unpaid internships also give you that much sought-after experience employers love to see. Your internship might even blossom into a job, like mine did.

When looking for internships, don't just look for anything. You want to do something that will further your career interests. If you're part of a club or organization, reach out and connect with some alumni. Ask the older members if they know of people that work in your field, and try to get an introduction.

You can also check with your school to see if they have a student help center that lets you apply for internships from local companies.

Many times, companies need to groom their next young professionals, or they may need some work done but not have the budget to hire someone full-time. These companies contact schools to post internships. Some universities have an online system that matches your resume with job skills provided by the company.

Some companies offer the same internships each semester, and you can usually get school credit for them too. These can be pretty good experiences, but I wouldn't pin high hopes on a job offer afterward. Companies that post the same recurring internships have created a niche for interns and may or may not hire you once your time is up.

You might have luck trying smaller companies and boutique agencies. You'll find the culture is very different with smaller companies as opposed to larger ones.

Large companies have a lot of rules and regulations that have come about from years of trial and error. They tend to be process-heavy, and usually the decision makers are far removed from the line workers. This isn't the case with a small business.

In smaller businesses, the generals are in the trenches with the troops. There are fewer employees, so you might even have direct access to the owner/CEO. So if the company has never had an intern before, you'll have a better chance of talking to someone that can bring you on board. Communication happens a little more quickly with fewer channels to go through, and you can be assured your hard work and creativity will be more visible to the people that make the decisions.

This isn't to say small companies are good and big ones are bad. If you can get an internship at a big company, that's great too. There are advantages to both. The more time you spend at a company, the more you'll come to know what works and what doesn't. That sort of knowledge will separate you from the pack when it's time to start a career.

If you're deciding to find a paid internship, you may have some trouble. Paid internships can be more competitive. They have all the benefits of unpaid internships, plus you get paid. That's hard to beat. A lot of students like you are looking for those same opportunities. Not to mention, there are far more unpaid internships than paid ones. You shouldn't let that stop you though. If you don't apply, you can never succeed.

A lot of intern programs will offer college credit in return for your work, so you can take one less class during the semester. If at all possible, find an internship relevant to your major. At the very least, you can find one that looks interesting, and try to find a way to get credit for it. No matter what, you'll get the same experience.

As an intern, you're going to get a lot of simple work to do. Hopefully you'll have ample opportunity to hone your skill set, but everyone has to take out the garbage sometime. If at the end of the semester you find you still loved it, then you know that's the career for you. If you couldn't stand it, then you have learned what you don't want to do. That can be invaluable. That's the sort of thing you won't find out in a classroom.

When you do land an internship, look at the people whose jobs you'd want. Notice their countenance. Are they happy? Are they overworked? Are they stressed out constantly? Talk to these people over lunch and get to know them. Ask if they like the lifestyle. Do not focus on pay so much because chasing money won't make you happy. You should make enough to make a living and love what you do.

Remember that not every valuable experience is labeled as an internship. Colleges offer many programs for different majors. These usually occur over the summer or off semester, but check with your academic department to see what they offer. A lot of times, Universities have access to important people that you wouldn't otherwise get to meet. Don't pass this opportunity up.

Scams

Not everything you find is legitimate. You have to be careful. There are a lot of jobs that target college students that may or may not work for you. Some of these jobs are scams. Sad to say there will always be some people trying to take advantage of you. You need to be able to tell the genuine opportunities from the scams. Here are a few good things to know:

An employer cannot legally ask you your age or income. You don't have to answer those questions in an interview. The employer has the right to know if you can commit to a certain schedule, nothing more. An employer also cannot ask you if you have a car—only if you have reliable transportation.

You should never take a job from someone you never meet in person. The only exception I'd put here is if you're interviewing for a job out of town. Then you should at least to a video call, but even then you need to be wary. Always research companies that contact you before you agree to anything. Even popular sites like Monster.com have scammers on there because there is no such thing a full-proof policing system.

If someone contacts you regarding a job at their company, visit the company's website. If it's the real deal, chances are your contact will include the site in his email signature. If it's not there, do a search. If you have a hard time finding it, then that should be a red flag.

If you do find their site and it looks suspect (poorly designed, like it's from the early 90's, and there are a lot of typos) search the better business bureau's site for their listing. http://www.bbb.org. Remember, just because a company puts one of these images on their site, does not mean they actually registered:

Never take a job where the only requirement is that you exchange money from one account to another. Also, don't give your employer your bank account number unless you're absolutely sure it's a legitimate business and the reason they need it is for direct deposit.

When you get a job, you only have to show a driver's license or state ID and your social security card (they need it for tax purposes).

If you have a bad feeling about something, don't go through with it. The right opportunities are out there if you keep looking. Don't take anything out of desperation or because you believe nothing else will come along. Have faith and confidence in yourself, and you'll be fine.

Chapter 11

Invest in Yourself

For the last chapter, I want to leave you with something that will carry you through anything in life: the right mindset. The right mindset is key to success, happiness, you name it. If you can start thinking of yourself as an investment, everything you do starts to align to grow your abilities and competence. You are your greatest asset. You are the source of your livelihood, and that will never change. College is an investment; classes are an investment; books are an investment. You pay money now in the belief that the benefit will one day pay it back and more, but there is another valuable resource you pay, except you can never get it back: time.

Even if you spend a lot of time doing hobbies and volunteer work, it always helps to re-evaluate your choices. Remember that you have access to the most incredible resource ever developed: the Internet. Your ambition isn't limited to the number of books in a library. You can hop on Facebook or Twitter and follow a personal hero. You can search for a book on any subject and have it shipped to you or download it immediately. You can read blogs and articles about successful people that are doing what you want to do.

Investing in yourself means taking advantage of each opportunity you have. Don't overlook anything as unimportant. You have no idea what experiences you'll need to prepare you for the next step in your life. Each class, each college job, each activity you participate in will give you experience, and you may find that down the road, you have the edge. Don't rule out any classes or internships as pointless.

I once took a course I never got credit for. In my final semester in college, I wanted to take a course on entrepreneurship. Both of my parents owned their own businesses, and it was something I could see myself doing. On top of that, the course wasn't taught by a professor of economics or anything like that: it was taught by an adjunct, an actual business owner. How could I pass up the opportunity to learn from someone who did this for a living?

I show up to class to find out it's full, so I was wait-listed. Well by the third week, enough people dropped out so that I could officially "join" the class (though I had been going since day 1). Turns out, the last day to add a class had already passed.

It didn't matter though. I wasn't in this class for the credit. I wanted the experience of having taken this class. I stayed with it the entire semester and did well. Having gotten the knowledge I was after, I graduated and went on. If you look at my transcripts, you won't see that class anywhere, but who cares? I believe I'm a better person for learning what I did, and that's the mentality you should have.

At the end of the day, if you think a piece of paper is a substitute for ambition and hard, practical knowledge, you're dead wrong.

The more experiences you have in school, and the more you challenge yourself, the better prepared you will be for the real world. Bosses will expect more out of you than anyone has before:

> *"If you think your teacher is tough, wait till you get a boss."* - Bill Gates

In the workforce, the focus is not on you and your success—it is about the success of the company. If you want to move up, you must take the extra step. Make yourself invaluable. Show initiative and dedication. These are investments of your time that can pay off in a promotion later. Nobody will hand you anything.

> *"Be a yardstick of quality. Some people aren't used to an environment where excellence is expected."* - Steve Jobs

When you take the extra time and go the extra mile, you position yourself for opportunity to find you, no matter where you are on the corporate ladder.

I worked at a restaurant for quite some time. After turning 21, I wanted to become a bartender; they made better money and generally seemed to have a better time at work. But the managers didn't want to take the time to have me trained.

One night, I show up and find out they had too many servers scheduled. A manager asks me if I'd like to serve in the bar, and rather than take the night off, I agreed. I approached the bartender to ask if he'd train me. He agreed, and I ran the idea by the managers. They didn't have a problem with it.

During the course of the night, another bartender came in to check the schedule, and offered to train me on opening the bar the next morning. I wasn't supposed to come in. I ask permission from the managers, and once again, I trained in the bar. Two more sessions, and I was ready, but there wasn't room for another bartender in the rotation.

Not more than one week passed before two bartenders didn't make it to work and didn't call in, an automatic dismissal. While the managers were panicking and discussing what to do, I show up. After that busy Friday night, not only was I a bartender, I also had the choicest shifts: Friday and Saturday night.

At the time, I had no intention of remaining in the restaurant business for the rest of my life, but I made the opportunity, got the experience, and was rewarded with a position I wanted. The job was more enjoyable; I made more money, and I got to watch ESPN in the bar.

Yes, working up to bartender isn't that exciting, but if you learn one thing from that story it's this: do more than the minimum. Take that extra step nobody else will, even if there's no guarantee of payoff. You never know when opportunity will present itself, but you want to make sure you are ready when it does.

Investing in yourself simply means that you dedicate your extra time and extra money to getting closer to your goals. Goals change, priorities change, but the ability to achieve is a skill you will have forever. Commit yourself to excellence, and just keep trying. You will soon find that you can do more than you ever imagined.

The Art of Learning

Learning is an active pursuit, not a passive one. You have to take action and be unafraid to make mistakes. Taking on something new shouldn't be easy. If it is, it's not something worth learning.

When you want to master something, the first thing you need to do is visualize what success will look like. It's a self-fulfilling prophecy. Envision success, and you will eventually become successful. See failure, and you'll find it harder to achieve.

Once you know what your end goal is, you set out to master it. Mastery won't happen right away, and sometimes it will feel like you're moving backwards. Don't worry, that's all a part of the learning process:

Stage One: Observation. Watch someone else do what you want to master. You mentally record as much information as possible so that you can move on to Stage Two.

Stage Two: Mimicry. You recreate the skill performed to the best of your ability.

Stage Three: Refinement. You refine the skill slowly so that you can do it perfectly at least once.

Stage Four: Repetition. Once you're able to do a skill fundamentally perfectly, you repeat it over and over again so that it becomes second nature.

Stage Five: Fall-out. This happens regardless of the skill, and this occurs especially so when trying to memorize or remember study material. You temporarily forget or lose the ability to do the skill perfectly. You end up having to concentrate harder to overcome this stage.

Stage Six: Mastery. You have now memorized and mastered the skill so that you can do it almost effortlessly.

Noel Burch categorized human learning into four stages. His model is called the Four Stages of Competence.

Stage One: Unconscious Incompetence. You don't know what you don't know. At the very outset, there is so much about this new skill that you don't know. You may not realize its true importance or difficulty.

Stage Two: Conscious Incompetence. You've spent some time trying to learn this new skill, and you realize that it's not as easy as you once thought. You now have a clearer picture of what it will take to master this skill.

Stage Three: Conscious Competence. You know how to do the skill, but it still requires a good degree of concentration and focus.

Stage Four: Unconscious Competence. You can do the skill perfectly without even thinking about it. You have achieved mastery.

The Climb to Success

Success is a lot like hiking Mount Everest. You see these people on TV and think how great it would be to be one of those people, but you just can't imagine how they got there. Those people are in shape. They've been climbing for a long time, and they know what they're doing. But you're looking at the end result of all of their hard work. Those climbers took the opportunities available to them. They didn't rest and let the world pass them by as their dreams got farther and farther away. They started just like everyone else—with dozens of failures followed by small victories. You'll never see the full journey on a show.

So no matter what you may see, never believe you can't. You will create what you believe. Start with the assumption that you are successful. Have confidence and don't be afraid of failure. Failure, after all, is just another step on the path to the summit.

Everest is one of the most dangerous environments on Earth. Violent storms form from nowhere. Year after year climbers are forced to travel back down the mountain and wait it out. Some of those people have to go home, hopefully to come back another time and conquer the mountain, but not always. Others wait out the storm and make it to the top.

Reaching the summit is never a straight climb. A lot of climbers move up and down the mountain several times before attempting the summit. Success then, isn't always straightforward. Sometimes you have to climb down before you can rise up. You have to believe in yourself and hold on to that belief like it's your life force.

So when someone says that achievement is a choice, they are right. There are countless things in the world that will stand in your way and tell you that you can't, but the most threatening, debilitating, and insidious foe is yourself. You have to fight for your place, but if you can't defeat self-doubt, you cannot hope to overcome external challenges.

A warning though: don't confuse choice with want. Everybody wants to succeed. Simply wanting is not enough: you have to need to succeed. Choice implies action; to choose is an active verb, not a state of being. Choosing to be successful isn't as easy as waking up and saying "I'm going to do it!" That's just stating intent—the choice comes when you take steps to fulfill that intent.

Wake up in the morning with a clear goal in mind. Set aside time to meet that goal. Make it a priority. A fairly common goal is to exercise and eat healthy. These are great habits to pick up because they fuel your other successes. Keeping healthy gives you energy and releases endorphins. You feel better about yourself and your life. Set aside time every day to exercise. Even if you only do it three times a week, keep to it. More energy means more drive, which leads to faster success. A healthy diet will also keep your mind sharp. A poor diet will rob you of vitality and focus. Remember: garbage in, garbage out.

You also need to befriend successful people. They will push you to do better. The saying, "Birds of a feather flock together," has truth to it. As human beings, we are social animals that want acceptance. When you surround yourself with deadbeats, losers, and bad influences, you're more likely to engage in their type of behaviors to get their acceptance. If you associate with movers and shakers, you're much more likely to do something worthwhile. Picking the right friends in college can drastically change your next four years for the better.

Surround yourself with inspiration. Incorporate a healthy habit into your daily routine, and be fanatical about it. Read inspirational stories, follow inspirational people. Learn better habits from those who have come before you. Whether you recite a personal motto while staring into the mirror, or put up an inspirational poster in your room, don't let these things lose meaning for you.

It's not easy breaking bad habits, and it's not easy making new ones. You have to dedicate yourself to it. Not everyone will understand your desire to change. Those people won't readily understand or encourage you. You have to know that what you're doing is necessary for you to get where you want to be. Explain it to your family, and try to get their support. It's tough making big changes alone. Everyone needs a kick in the butt now and again. Building a network of support will only make your success that much more inevitable.

Don't set out to totally change yourself overnight. Change takes time. Just worry about meeting your daily goals. Day by day, you'll form a habit of success. Don't worry if you slip up once in a while. You will fail, but so does everyone. The truly successful, the real champions are the ones that bull through their failures. They learn from what went wrong and avoid those mistakes the next time around. If you can't move beyond the failure, if you refuse to accept your mistakes for what they are—then nothing will change for you. If you aren't happy doing what you are doing now, then you must become the change you desire.

From Humble Beginnings

I once heard a quote about how Michael Jordan became such a great basketball player. What really stuck in my head was this one line: "He's failed more times than you've even tried." I'm paraphrasing a little, but that is such a powerful thought. I remember hearing about other famous people that failed many times before they became renowned. I want to share some of those stories with you.

Ulysses S. Grant – best known as the Union general who defeated General Lee of the Confederacy, Grant later became the 18th president of the United States. Before he became General, he attempted several business ventures in Missouri that all failed. Imagine if his failure stopped him from going on and becoming one of the most popular military names of the Civil War.

Thomas Edison – the inventor that gave us the light bulb, made 1,000 prototypes before finally making the one that worked. What would have happened if he had given up?

Winston Churchill – Britain's famous Prime Minister, who once said, "Never give in, never give in, never, never, never, never - in nothing, great or small, large or petty - never give in except to convictions of honor and good sense. Never, Never, Never, Never give up" failed the sixth grade and never won public office before becoming Prime Minister.

Henry Ford – famous for his car company and inventing the assembly line, he went broke five times before making the first car.

R.H. Macy – he founded Macy's, which failed seven times before it finally survived in New York City.

Robert Goddard – the scientific community rejected his ideas on the grounds that rocket propulsion would not work in outer space.

Babe Ruth – he held records for the most home runs and the most strikeouts.

Abraham Lincoln – he lost the election for state legislature, Congress, the Senate, and the vice-presidency before becoming the 16th president of the United States.

Imagine what little history we'd have if everyone avoided success for fear of failure. That's the real key: be confident; be fearless; be relentless.

Conclusion

Thanks for reading my book. We've covered a lot of ground, and I hope you've found something valuable. A lot of these lessons I learned the hard way, and after speaking with a lot of different people, I realized I wasn't alone.

By now, you are better prepared to write a great application. You have learned critical writing and process skills, and can put to use several of the frameworks we discussed for time management and prioritization, like CARVER and Pareto's Law.

You've gotten to see real responses from major Universities to questions asked by high school students. Hopefully you've reflected a bit on yourself and have a better idea of what college will be the right fit for you.

The chapter on paying for school should have given you plenty of ideas for finding money to pay for school. Make use of the efficiency hacks we've discussed, and find others that work for you. Let me know what you discover.

Be sure to visit my website: austinfadely.com for some useful tools you can download for free and use.

If you have any thoughts or ideas about what we've discussed, I'd love to hear from you.

Email me at the address below, follow my Facebook page, or send me a Tweet @austinfadely.

-Austin Fadely

austinfadely@gmail.com

http://austinfadely.com

https://www.facebook.com/conquering-college

Appendix A

Interview Answers by University

Duke University

I see that your typical applicant has significant extra-curricular commitments. Can a person who has little to no extra-curricular activities expect a good chance of being accepted? What if the student activities are self-lead, meaning outside of an organization?

> The kind of extracurricular activity—as long as it's a meaningful one, worth doing—is less relevant than the commitment and impact it embodies. We're looking for people who make a difference, who leave an organization, place, or activity better than they found it. That can take place in an almost infinite number of venues. It's also possible that a student have an impact that is entirely academic or intellectual, not extracurricular. Those people are rare, but equally valued in the admissions process.

How far does knowing a foreign language go in getting accepted to a University?

Typically our applicants take a minimum of five academic courses a year—English, history/social studies, math, science, and a foreign language. Duke also has a foreign language requirement for the degree, so significant exposure to the language of another culture is clearly important to us. There would have to be a compelling reason for a student not to be taking a foreign language in high school. It's quite rare among our applicants.

What do you look for in a good admissions essay? Is it more important to be grammatically correct or engaging? How would you rate an essay that is mechanically correct but dull/irrelevant?

We look for something well written that tells us something about the applicant and that reflects good thinking. It's all three of those qualities together that make for a good essay.

Are there any pet peeves you have when seeing poor applications?

Lack of effort in filling out the application. That's really the only thing that rubs me the wrong way.

Are previously rejected applications given equal consideration for the next term (assuming the student resubmits the same application)?

We admit students only for the fall, so this question doesn't really apply to us.

I see you accept both the ACT and SAT, would it benefit a student to take both or does it matter?

It's entirely the student's choice. It doesn't matter to us.

What is the most important character trait an applicant should have? I see your website mentions the ambitious and the curious; how would these traits separate an applicant from the rest of her peers?

> The most important character trait is integrity; without that nothing else matters. But assuming the integrity is there, we look for strong academic and intellectual ability, the inclination to take advantage of opportunities, and the willingness to be a contributing member of a diverse and interesting community of talented individuals. Students with these characteristics, who reveal in their applications that they will offer something valuable to the community and benefit from being part of that community often find themselves with lots of good choices when it comes to the college admissions process. It's difficult to describe exactly how one student distinguishes himself or herself in a pool of almost 30,000 applicants.

How big of a role does the personal recommendation letter play in the application? Is there anything you would tell a student about whom to ask to recommend him? For example, should a student choose someone who has known him the longest or someone he's had more contact with in the past few years?

> We look for insight from letters of recommendation, particularly with respect to the kind of student someone is. I tell students that

they should get letters of recommendations from the teachers for whom they've done their best work.

Is there any general advice you have for college applicants? Or if there is anything you feel I did not address, please let me know.

Students should love every college on their list. Don't apply to a school you don't want to attend. College admissions is full of so much uncertainty now, make sure that every college you're applying to is one you'd be happy to attend.

Email Interview conducted on August 8th, 2011 with Christoph Guttentag, Dean of Undergraduate Admissions at Duke University. Interview published with permission from Mr. Guttentag.

Florida State University

Can a person who has little to no extra-curricular activities expect a good chance of being accepted?

> While it is possible to be accepted to Florida State University with little or no extracurricular activities, the typical student that we admit is both academically strong and socially engaged.

How far does knowing a foreign language go in getting accepted to a University?

> Two sequential units of the same foreign language are required for admission to Florida State; however, we prefer students to challenge themselves by taking additional years of the same foreign language.

What do you look for in a good admissions essay? Is it more important to be grammatically correct or engaging?

> Both grammar and engagement are necessary. An essay can be engrossing but may lose my attention if it is riddled with spelling or grammatical errors.

Are there any pet peeves you have when seeing poor applications?

> A sloppy application is my biggest pet peeve. If the student does not care, why should I? In addition, we correspond to our students by email. I would recommend students having a separate

email account for the application process. Some of the email addresses are just not appropriate for the application process.

Are previously rejected applications given equal consideration for the next term?

We will reconsider all applicants who apply for another term. I would hope they would submit additional documentation.

Does it look better to take both the ACT and SAT, or does it matter?

We recommend that applicants take both exams since we use the best composite/total score for admission purposes.

What is the most important character trait an applicant should have?

We would hope all of our applicants would be honest, well-round individuals who embrace leadership, learning, service, and global awareness. In fact, our essay question on the application addresses this – "Florida State University is more than just a world-class academic institution preparing you for a future career. We are a caring community of well-rounded individuals who embrace leadership, learning, service, and global awareness. With this in mind, which of these characteristics appeal most to you, and why."

How big of a role do recommendation letters play in the application? Is there anything you would tell a student about whom to ask to recommend him/her?

Letters of recommendation are not required and will not be used in the decision-making process.

Is there any general advice you have for college applicants? Or if there is anything you feel I did not address, please let me know.

Preparation for the college application process does not begin in the senior year. It starts as early as middle school when selecting challenging courses and progressing through high school with a rigorous course schedule. There is no need to apply to 10-15 colleges. Do your research to determine what you really want in your future college and apply to schools that are a good fit. As all colleges will emphasize, "It's a match to be made, not a prize to be won." And finally celebrate all the acceptances with your family, and don't take the "no's" personally.

Email Interview conducted on June 30th, 2011 with Janice Finney, Director of Admissions at Florida State University. Interview published with permission from Ms. Finney.

Oklahoma State University

Can a person who has little to no extra-curricular activities expect a good chance of being accepted?

> As a public institution, OSU's admission standards are determined by the Oklahoma State Regents for Higher Education (OSRHE). The admission requirements for the 2011-2012 academic year, as approved by OSRHE, are:

> Option 1: ACT 24 or SAT 1090

> Option 2: High School GPA of an unweighted 3.0 and is in the top 33.3% rank of their class.

> Option 3: High School GPA in the 15 unit core is a 3.0 and has a score of 21 ACT or 980 SAT

> Option 4: High School GPA in the 15 unit core is a 3.0 or 22 ACT or 1020 SAT and answers to the application/scholarship questions.

> https://admissions.okstate.edu/admission-requirements

How far does knowing a foreign language go in getting accepted to a University?

> Oklahoma State University requires all students to complete a 15-unit core curricular requirement for admission. In the "Other"

section highlighted below, students have the option to utilize a foreign language or computer science course to meet the 15-unit requirement.

SUBJECTS	YEARS
English (grammar, composition & literature)	4
Mathematics (algebra I & above)	3
History & Citizenship (American history required, plus additional units from economics, geography, government, history, or non-Western culture)	3
Laboratory Science	3
Other (from any of the above or foreign language or computer science)	2

https://admissions.okstate.edu/admission-requirements#freshmen

What do you look for in a good admissions essay? Is it more important to be grammatically correct or engaging?

OSU's admission and scholarship questions from the application for admission are used to award certain scholarships as well as help determine holistic and alternative admission candidates.

These questions allow applicants to highlight their involvement in school, work, community service, and other organizations. It is important applicants demonstrate their best possible writing ability both in content and grammar, however, community involvement and demonstrated and potential leadership skills are also evaluated.

https://admissions.okstate.edu/sites/default/files/files/Publicati ons/Application.pdf

Are there any pet peeves you have when seeing poor applications?

At OSU, we are available to work closely with students to make sure they submit a completed application file as well as showcase their abilities and potential. A completed application file includes:

- Completed admission/scholarship application

- $40 non-refundable application fee or waiver

- Official high school transcript or college transcript when applicable

- ACT test score or SAT test score when applicable

- Complete admission/scholarship questions

https://admissions.okstate.edu/sites/default/files/files/Publicati ons/Application.pdf

Are previously rejected applications given equal consideration for the next term?

> Oklahoma State University does not review rejected applications automatically for the next term. However, Oklahoma State University does encourage applicants to resubmit an updated application for admission if he or she is interested in applying for the next term.

Does it look better to take both the ACT and SAT, or does it matter?

> Oklahoma State University requires the following documentation for freshman admission; a completed admission/scholarship application, $40 non-refundable application fee, an official high school transcript, and an ACT or SAT test score. While we typically encourage students to retest when they have only tested once and are bordering admission criteria or remediation and assessment criteria, we do not advocate excessive testing. Students can often better showcase their ability by retesting after additional semesters of work are completed.
>
> https://admissions.okstate.edu/admission-requirements#freshmen

What is the most important character trait an applicant should have?

> There is rarely one particular trait an applicant should have, however we encourage students to showcase their academic as well as leadership abilities and potential. By revealing more than

scholarly abilities, a student can showcase other interests, which may lead to scholarly pursuits, study abroad, campus life or research interests during his or her academic career.

How big of a role do recommendation letters play in the application? Is there anything you would tell a student about whom to ask to recommend him/her?

Oklahoma State University encourages applicants to submit letters of recommendation, specifically to address areas in which there may be remediations. Recommendation letters should be written by representatives that the applicant has known for at least a year and that can address academic areas of concern. Letters of recommendation are used most often by the Admission Review Committee that evaluates students for holistic and alternative admission.

Is there any general advice you have for college applicants? Or if there is anything you feel I did not address, please let me know.

Work with your admissions counselor! We are here to help and look forward to working with prospective students and families throughout the process.

Email Interview conducted on September 13th, 2011 with Erin Smith, approved by Kari Aldredge, Associate Director of Undergraduate Admissions at Oklahoma State University. Interview published with permission from Ms. Smith and Ms. Aldredge.

University of Colorado: Boulder

Can a person who has little to no extra-curricular activities expect a good chance of being accepted?

> I think they do have a very good chance of being accepted. Part of the reason is that Admissions Counselors and professionals need to be very careful for making judgments they're not sure of. If somebody doesn't have a lot of ECs, we could make a judgment that they aren't involved, but we don't know the family dynamic. The student may have a significant responsibility in the home. Maybe they have to help raise family members, they have a job, or maybe they have an illness that precludes them from participating. I know many top academic students that do well in class but are light on the ECs. I'd love to have those students at the University of Colorado.

> One of the things we talk about at UC, we want to look for a good student and a good citizen. What I mean by that is not only being involved in the high school or community, but also to make it a better place or are doing meaningful things in their life outside of the classroom, whether through organized activities or not.

How far does knowing a foreign language go in getting accepted to a University?

It's an important part for us at University of Colorado Boulder, and it's written into our admissions standards. There is a minimum of 2 years, and we encourage students to have that and more of a foreign language. We believe in a global community.

What do you look for in a good admissions essay? Is it more important to be grammatically correct or engaging?

Both. The reason is we really are looking for students to show us strong examples of their writing capabilities. Sentence structure, grammar, punctuation, and themes are all critical elements in the review of an essay. The student also has to be able to get their point across.

Some schools will ask a very direct question on the essay. In that case, we're looking for how well the student formulated their ideas and put them into paragraphs. There is also a free-form writing example, and I think there is a lot of opportunity to go a lot of different directions. The biggest mistake students make in the essay is when they try to write what they think we want to read. We find that students write about a subject that's important to them, those turn out to be the most compelling essays we like to read.

Are there any pet peeves you have when seeing poor applications?

No and yes. I think the thing that is sometimes concerning is when a University is asking a set of very important questions about who a student is. In our essay, we talk about the importance of diversity in higher education. There are so many kinds of diversity, not just racial, but geographic and academic. If you are going to join a community that values diversity, it looks bad when you spend little or no time addressing that. It's disconcerting because that's somebody we're looking to make part of our student body.

When the application is put together very quickly or without much thought, admissions officers would find that a concern. If students are interested in joining our campus community, we want to know the questions are worth their time and effort. It's rushing and hurrying through this process that's the biggest concern.

Fortunately now that applications are online, problems such as illegibility, stains etc are disappearing.

Another thing we want students to do is for them to realize it's a business relationship with the college, not a social one. You have to make sure your communication style is professional. The application is a time to be more formal.

We get email addresses that are very revealing. There are email addresses that can be used in the social environment with your friends, but when we don't know the applicant, we prefer to see a more professional email address. You're submitting documents to an individual you may not have met, so it's best to put your best foot forward.

Are previously rejected applications given equal consideration for the next term?

We don't automatically reconsider applications, but each new submitted application is considered fresh. A lot of times we try to work with a student to outline steps for him to gain admission to the University. To students who are reapplying, we think that is outstanding, and we certainly want to help them, and a lot of times there is new academic material in the application.

Does it look better to take both the ACT and SAT, or does it matter?

We are very clear that we don't have a preference. We take either, but if we were to provide advice, we recommend they take both because they are different tests. One test may fit a student's style better and she may be more comfortable with it. We leave that to the student since there is no preference. We consider the highest score.

The other thing that college admissions officers are doing when they are looking at an application, they are looking for a reason to admit rather than a reason to deny, so we want to give a student credit for the higher score.

What is the most important character trait an applicant should have?

I can't single out the most important, but here are several: honor, integrity, appreciating similarities and differences between people, and someone who is academically engaged are four traits we are continually looking for. We are also looking for someone who gives back to their community. We want to see someone who knows the world is bigger than their sphere.

If it came down to one trait, it would be academic preparedness. We don't want students to come here for a semester or a year and leave, we want them to come here and graduate. So the ability to assess academic preparedness in the classroom would probably lead the way.

How big of a role do recommendation letters play in the application? Is there anything you would tell a student about whom to ask to recommend him/her?

Pick the faculty member that can really speak to your ability to succeed in college. We've seen students pick the most difficult subjects and the teachers that go with that, with the idea that if they pick the toughest subject it will be more impressive. That person may not be able to write as well about the student than another faculty member that has known that student for a long time. Sometimes students make that mistake of analyzing who they want to write their letters for them and picking the appropriate individual.

The other mistake students will sometimes make is not giving their teachers enough time to write a good letter. Students should always give their faculty members ample time. The faculty member has a lot of priorities, and if you give her only two days to write a letter for you, she shouldn't give you much effort. If you give her a few weeks, a copy of your resume, and other achievements, so she is prepared and has enough time to write you a really good letter.

Is there any general advice you have for college applicants? Or if there is anything you feel I did not address, please let me know.

The only advice I would give is to find a way to manage the time that the application process takes. I'm not just referring to the admission application. Students are so busy, then they hit their final year, they have all these applications and financial aid and scholarships. Then they have to fill out housing applications and orientation forms. It can be a lot of hurried paperwork if you don't manage your time.

Get an early start, and keep on top of the deadlines; you can dial down the anxiety in the whole process.

Email Interview conducted on July 5th, 2011 with Kevin MacLennan, Director of Admissions at University of Colorado: Boulder Interview published with permission from Mr. MacLennan.

The University of Hawai'i at Mānoa

Can a person who has little to no extra-curricular activities expect a good chance of being accepted?

> Yes. The admissions committee primarily looks at academic course work, cumulative grade point average and test scores. Letters of recommendation and personal essays that may include information about a student's extracurricular activities might be mentioned but these documents are not required as part of the application.

How far does knowing a foreign language go in getting accepted to a University?

> One of our admission requirements asks that student have four (4) college-prep courses. This can include a foreign language but is not a requirement for admission.

What do you look for in a good admissions essay? Is it more important to be grammatically correct or engaging?

> Admissions essays are not required but welcomed as part of the application. If a student does submit one, both grammar and content of the essay will be evaluated.
>
> Admissions essays that highlight the student's academic ability, maturity, and experience are valued. Students who show initiative

is equally as impressive because it shows critical thinking. Essays that also include a list of what they would like to do once they finish college and how their degree will help them achieve their goals indicates that they have done their research and shows genuine interest in applying to our University.

Since the essay is a reflection of the student's writing ability and personality, it is extremely important that the student use proper grammar and spelling. It also reflects the time the student spent writing and proof-reading the essay before submission.

Are there any pet peeves you have when seeing poor applications?

Personally, some of my pet peeves are illegible handwriting, unprofessional e-mails addresses (i.e. ilovevideogames@hotmail.com versus having their first and last name), and essays that have not been proof-read and are not personalized to the school (i.e. writing, "Dear Princeton" when it is being sent to University of Hawai'i at Mānoa). I should note however, that although these are "pet peeves" they do not affect a student's admissibility to the University.

Are previously rejected applications given equal consideration for the next term?

Yes, students are given a fair evaluation and have a chance to appeal decisions as long as they have improved academically or have changed something in their application. For example, if a student raises their GPA or has improved test scores, we can re-consider the application. The student will have to submit the new documents and a statement to have the admission committee re-evaluate the file. It must be noted however, that students applying for another term must submit another application packet.

Does it look better to take both the ACT and SAT, or does it matter?

The University of Hawai'i at Mānoa has no preference to either test, we will accept both. However, for the ACT, students must take the writing category to be considered.

Also, if the student takes the test multiple times (either the SAT or ACT), we will take the highest score in each category. For example, if a student scores a 500/510/530 on the SAT the first time and a 520/540/510 the second time, we will report scores as 520/540/530.

What is the most important character trait an applicant should have?

Self-initiative. Students who take control of their own application show the student's maturity and desire to attend the University and something THEY want and not an influence of anyone else (parents, teachers, friends, etc).

How big of a role do recommendation letters play in the application? Is there anything you would tell a student about whom to ask to recommend him/her?

> Although letters of recommendation are not required, they can help strengthen an application. They do not guarantee admission for students but can definitely help us better understand the applicant. Letters of recommendation can be most beneficial to a student if there is an area in which they are lacking. For example, if a student scores low on the math portion of the SAT but performs better in the classroom, a letter from a math teacher that can highlight the student's ability can help.

Is there any general advice you have for college applicants? Or if there is anything you feel I did not address, please let me know.

> My advice to students is to take every opportunity to learn something about college and the schools that they are interested in. Attend college fairs, high school visits, take a campus tour and attend special events sponsored by the University. If possible, do this early. The more experience the student has, the better they can make a decision on where you want to go and what will be the right fit.

> I also highly encourage asking questions, no matter how big or small. College is an opportunity to change and create a new and exciting future for one's self. If a student does not ask questions, they will not get the answers and will not learn and learning is what college is all about!

Email Interview conducted on April 26th, 2011 with Abigail Huliganga, Admissions Counselor at the University of Hawai'i at Mānoa. Interview published with permission from Ms. Huliganga.

University of Maryland: Baltimore County

We should include somewhere before answering these questions that there is not a "one size fits all" approach to the college admissions process. Each admissions review committee evaluates applications differently depending on the size of the institution, university goals, economic factors, student body, and a myriad of other factors. I would recommend the student to meet with the admissions counselor from their school of choice. Admissions counselors are there to assist students with the application process along with alleviate some anxiety that this process may cause. The student will find that admissions counselors are transparent in what their respective school is looking for in an applicant and will provide the best advice to direct the student towards academic success. The challenge from the students prospective is asking the right questions to guide the conversation. Lastly, while it seems simple, read the application requirements, the school will ask for exactly what they require from the applicant.

Can a person who has little to no extra-curricular activities expect a good chance of being accepted?

> It depends on the institution. There are a couple of scenarios to take into consideration: Student A, who has no extra-curricular activity but does well academically and student B who has a myriad of extra-curricular activities and average grades. For student A, imagine if every student who applied to "blank" university had a 4.5 weighted gpa and a 2400 SAT? The question

to ask is what distinguishes this student from the other applicants? Also take into consideration for student A limited availability of seats for the incoming freshman class. If student A applied to an institution where limited enrollment does not exist, then student A would be a prime candidate.   For student B, generally speaking, extra-curricular activities are looked upon favorably; however, extra-curricular activities do not replace subpar grades.

How far does knowing a foreign language go in getting accepted to a University?

For most institutions, a foreign language is not "required" to gain admission into the university. Keep in mind if the student is applying to a liberal arts institution, there is a language requirement to graduate from the university. In that vein, it is beneficial to the student to have high school foreign language experience so that he/she may be able to test out or test into a higher level language class to complete the language requirement sooner. On the other hand, if a student is applying directly to a foreign affairs program at "blank" institution, having language proficiency may be mandatory for admission. It is also important to address students with documented learning disabilities. If the student has an IEP in high school that exempted the student from taking a foreign language, an exception can be made at the post secondary level.

What do you look for in a good admissions essay? Is it more important to be grammatically correct or engaging?

> In a college admissions essay, it is important for the student to stay on topic and present a grammatically sound essay. Essentially, the essay gives prospective students the opportunity to demonstrate academic talent beyond a gpa and test score. Different institutions place different weighting on the essay. For some institutions, the essay accounts for 30 percent of the admissions review process and in others it may only account for 5 percent. To add another layer to the essay, aside from general admissions, some schools offer honors and scholars programs along with select scholarship opportunities. For these opportunities, the essay can become increasingly significant as certain courses in the above programs may be writing intensive and the committee members are looking for a success predictor.

Are there any pet peeves you have when seeing poor applications?

> Pet Peeves, no as the admissions process has to remain objective and fair. However, I would like to stress the importance of putting accurate information on the application. For example, if the student does not know his/her social security number, he/she should double check before submitting the application. An incorrect social security number prevents admissions staff from matching appropriate documents with the student. This, in turn, can slow down the application review process.

Are previously rejected applications given equal consideration for the next term?

> The term equal consideration can be a little misleading. If the student applies and is not offered admission and the student does nothing differently, then, the student will not be offered admission for the next term. However, some institutions allow for the student to submit additional test scores or a final transcript (with a strong upward trend) for additional review. Sometimes, all the student has to do is demonstrate academic success at a post secondary institution for one semester and resubmit their interest in the original institution and can receive a favorable result.

Does it look better to take both the ACT and SAT, or does it matter?

> The SAT/ACTs are standardized tests recognized differently regionally. Please also keep in mind scores on these tests should be relatively, if not, the same. In fact, the College Board and ACT provide concordance charts that show the equivalent scores on the other exam and admissions offices usually find these scores to be comparable. Read the admissions requirements carefully because the application will say if the school prefers the SAT or ACT.

What is the most important character trait an applicant should have?

> In general, the strongest trait a student should have is the gift of

decision making. Rather than apply to 30 schools, students should thoroughly research 3 or 4 schools then the student will make the best use of his/her time and energy. Regarding the actual applicant, I would recommend that the student make a plan in high school to be the best he or she can be without excuses. As admissions professionals, we do not know the student personally so the student truly has to "look good on paper." While there are extenuating circumstances, "Sara just does not test well" is not a solid excuse to reverse an admission decision.

How big of a role do recommendation letters play in the application? Is there anything you would tell a student about whom to ask to recommend him/her?

For general admissions, letters of recommendation are reviewed as a part of the application. As with standardized tests, the institution will indicate on the application if letters of recommendation are optional or mandatory. When the student is applying to program specific majors, then letters of recommendation will play a bigger role in the selection process.

Is there any general advice you have for college applicants? Or if there is anything you feel I did not address, please let me know.

Email Interview conducted on February 11th, 2011 with Danielle Jolly, Admissions Counselor at the University of Maryland: Baltimore County. Interview published with permission from Ms. Jolly.

University of North Carolina

Can a person who has little to no extra-curricular activities expect a good chance of being accepted?

> We do like to see students who have done something outside of the classroom. We would never admit or deny a student based solely on one item. We look at the total application for each student. It's hard to make an admissions call on one question. Generally speaking we do like to see students doing something outside of the classroom, but it can vary. For instance, practicing an instrument, working, volunteering, etc.

How far does knowing a foreign language go in getting accepted to a University?

> For Carolina, we do require at least 2 years of study of a foreign language in high school. Most of our competitive applicants exceed this and take it all the way to their senior year.

What do you look for in a good admissions essay? Is it more important to be grammatically correct or engaging?

> We like to see that a student understands the rules of grammar. We do hope that they take some time to proofread or ask someone else to look it over. We love to see an engaging essay where the content is captivating. Each year, applicants continue to amaze us. It is incredible to see how far a student will take an

admissions essay whether it's about their academic interests or humor. We always love seeing humor.

Are there any pet peeves you have when seeing poor applications?

> Rather than focus on what we don't like to see, we prefer applications where students have taken the time to provide as much information as possible about themselves. We can tell if a student has waited until the last minute in terms of carelessness in spelling and grammar. We like to see applications that are thoughtfully prepared and really demonstrate an interest in Carolina.

Are previously rejected applications given equal consideration for the next term?

> If we aren't able to offer admissions, they won't be able to be accepted for a following cycle; however transfer applications are considered differently, in that we don't see if they applied before. Each application is a new start. Transfer admission is a lot less competitive because there are far fewer applications for each slot. We receive nearly 3000 transfer student applications for 800 slots rather than 24,000 new student applications for 4000 slots.

Does it look better to take both the ACT and SAT, or does it matter?

> We don't require that students take both. It's just one or the other. Some students take both and that's fine, but they will not

be given advantage over a student that took only one of the tests.

What is the most important character trait an applicant should have?

> It's hard to identify just one. We look for kindness and compassion, overall integrity. We don't value one over the other. Students amaze and surprise us with what they bring to the table. We like to see diverse experiences and a diverse outlook on life. It's hard to pin it down to one trait.

How big of a role do recommendation letters play in the application? Is there anything you would tell a student about whom to ask to recommend him/her?

> We require a teacher recommendation and a counselor statement. It's important to think carefully and select a teacher that has known them for some time and has a clear understanding of their academic potential. A teacher from a core academic area from English to Math would be best, but most importantly choose a teacher that knows you well.

Is there any general advice you have for college applicants? Or if there is anything you feel I did not address, please let me know.

> Don't wait until the last minute. We can tell when applications are thrown together. It's important to begin cultivating relationships with teachers now so you can get a great recommendation later. Don't wait until the last minute until the

essay. We generally post essay questions in the summer, so you can start now and begin practicing. Essay questions are published on our Website.

Phone Interview conducted on July 5th, 2011 with Ashley Memory, Senior Assistant Director of Admissions at the University of North Carolina, Chapel Hill. Interview published with permission from Ms. Memory.

Virginia Tech

Can a person who has little to no extra-curricular activities expect a good chance of being accepted? This would depend on the definition of the term "extra-curricular."

> At Virginia Tech, we are looking for applicants who can show they are able to handle a challenging high school course load (while making very good grades), as well as activities outside their school work. This does not mean the activities have to be school club or sports oriented – not all applicants have the luxury of time or money for certain activities. A student whose evening activity is a part-time job to help out with family expenses, or running the household in the evenings (such as dinner and child care for younger siblings while the parent or guardian works) would be looked upon as favorably as an applicant with a long list of clubs and organizations. We actively look for evidence that strong student applicants are not just leaving school in the afternoons and spending all their free time texting or on the Internet, as part of their college fit will require skills for spending time wisely, juggling free time and fun with keeping up with rigorous academic demands.

How far does knowing a foreign language go in getting accepted to a University?

> Because we do not require a foreign language as part of the

admissions criteria, not having a foreign language will not necessarily hurt a strong applicant's chances; however, we certainly favorably view applicants who have taken strong academic courses that will help them prepare for college, and a sequence of foreign language would look more favorable than several non-academic electives on a transcript. We also recommend that students take advantage of the courses (if available) while in high school since foreign language is a required subject for graduation from Virginia Tech and can be fulfilled by gaining sufficient credit while still in high school (which could potentially free their schedule up for other courses at Virginia Tech, if they are admitted).

What do you look for in a good admissions essay? Is it more important to be grammatically correct or engaging?

A strong applicant should be able to write a solid essay that is grammatically correct. While Virginia Tech does not require essays as part of the undergraduate admissions application, we strongly encourage applicants to take advantage of the optional personal statements (they can submit up to three, no more than 200 words each) to help us hear their "voice" in addition to the required transcripts and test scores. While we are not looking for a college-level paper in this section, basic grammar is expected, and improper usage such as texting abbreviations are not acceptable. Applicants who submit shoddy work are not showing their best side to the Admissions Committee, which will be making a decision on applicants based on all the information they submit with their file, so checking for grammar and running their writing through a spell-check before they submit the application is a minimum expectation. Applicants should keep in mind that admissions committee members will see thousands of essays during the year, so those who can stand out in a good way – engaging, clever, original – are presenting themselves in a favorable light. While a good personal statement will never compensate for poor academic criteria, it can certainly help an applicant who is average in the pool rise a little higher than those who didn't take the extra effort on this step.

Are there any pet peeves you have when seeing poor applications?

Students who do not follow instructions (miss deadlines, fail to check the online status page we provide them to be sure their transcripts and scores are received, etc.) and then ask for special treatment as a result take up a lot of our time. Misspelling words that high school seniors should know, and generally not showing that care was taken with their application materials are other problems we see often.

Are previously rejected applications given equal consideration for the next term?

Students who have been denied admission and then apply for a later term as transfer students are given equal consideration with all other applicants in the applicant pool for that term. We favorably view students who, after being denied as freshmen, work with us throughout their first year at college elsewhere on course choice and present high college grades. Students who check with us, work with us, and follow our transfer advising early in their first year elsewhere typically have a high rate of success when applying to transfer after a year or two at another accredited institution.

I see you accept both the ACT and SAT, would it benefit a student to take both or does it matter?

It really does not matter which, or how many, tests are taken (though we absolutely do *not* advise taking standardized tests too many times -- in other words, we would advise against a number of test sittings that are excessive for the student's finances and/or performance). We in no way penalize students for the number or type of tests taken and take care to use only the highest score of any section from any test. We do not have a preference for the ACT or SAT – either or both is fine. (If they do take both, we will consider all scores reported. In other words, we would take the highest Critical Reading from the SAT and the highest math from the ACT for use in an applicant's review, if those were the highest scores for the applicant in question.)

What is the most important character trait an applicant should have?

An applicant (who may possibly be a student in the future at our respective school) should be respectful!

How big of a role do recommendation letters play in the application? Is there anything you would tell a student about whom to ask to recommend him/her?

Virginia Tech does not require letters of recommendation, though a letter that is sent with the applicant's transcript is read as part of the application file. In general, we would advise students to choose an individual who is familiar with them as a student and who can provide informed insight into how that student would be likely to succeed at our university, though the top criteria that we consider for all applicants are high school curriculum, grades, and test scores.

Is there any general advice you have for college applicants? Or if there is anything you feel I did not address, please let me know.

Applicants should take care to note specific requirements (and due dates) for all of the various schools to which they are applying, as they can vary widely. We consider it the applicant's responsibility to keep up with each school's requirements, not the other way around. We assume that a student who is truly interested in attending our university will take the time and make an effort to follow our clear instructions.

Email Interview conducted on June 5th, 2011 with Amy Widner, Public

Relations Coordinator at the Office of Undergraduate Admissions at Virginia Tech. Interview published with permission from Ms. Widner.

Appendix B

Works Cited

Lorin, Janet. *Student Loan Interest Rates Rise for 2014-2015 School Year.* May 7, 2014. http://www.bloomberg.com/news/articles/2014-05-07/student-loan-interest-rates-rise-for-2014-2015-school-year (accessed April 15, 2015).

Robert Bozick, Stefanie DeLuca. "Better Late Than Never? Delayed Enrollment in the High School to College Transition." *Johns Hopkins University Website.* September 2005. http://krieger.jhu.edu/wp-content/uploads/sites/28/2012/02/SF-Proofs-2.pdf (accessed April 15, 2015).

U.S. Department of Education, National Center for Education Statistics. *Fast Facts: Tution Costs of Colleges and Universities.* n.d. http://nces.ed.gov/fastfacts/display.asp?id=76 (accessed April 15, 2015).

Appendix C

Links

Admissions Information

Common Application: http://www.commonapp.org

National Association for College Admission Counseling:
http://www.nacac.com

Choosing a College

All About College: http://allaboutcollege.com

College Confidential: http://collegeconfidential.com

Know How 2 Go: http://knowhow2go.com

My College Guide: http://mycollegeguide.org/guru

Next Step U: http://nextstepu.com

Choosing a Major

College Grazing: http://collegegrazing.com

College Trends: http://collegetrends.org

Princeton Review: http://princetonreview.com/colleges-majors.aspx

Credit Card Information

Card Hub: http://www.cardhub.com

Card Ratings: http://www.cardratings.com/studentcreditcards.html

Credit Cards for College Students: http://www.creditcards.com/college-students.php

FAFSA Related

EFC Calculator: http://calculators.collegetoolkit.com/college-calculators/rescalcefc.aspx

FAFSA: http://www.fafsa.ed.gov

Selective Service: http://www.sss.gov

Online Degrees

Get Educated: www.geteducated.com

Online Education Database: http://oedb.org

World Wide Learn: http://www.worldwidelearn.com/

Scam Detection

Better Business Bureau: http://www.bbb.org

Federal Trade Commission: www.ftc.gov/scholarshipscams

Scholarship Search

College Board: https://www.collegeboard.org/

College Scholarships: http://www.collegescholarships.org/

Fast Web: http://www.fastweb.com/

FinAid: http://www.finaid.org/

Know How 2 Go: http://knowhow2go.acenet.edu/

Scholarship Experts: http://www.scholarshipexperts.com/

Scholarships.com: https://www.scholarships.com/

Scholarships and Contests

American Legion Oratorical Contest:
http://www.legion.org/oratorical/about

Ayn Rand Essay Contest: https://www.aynrand.org/students/essay-contests

Best Buy (via Cappex): https://www.cappex.com/scholarship/listings/Best-Buy-Scholarship-Program/-s-d-2673

Buick Achievers Program: http://www.buickachievers.com

Coca-Cola Scholars: http://www.coca-colascholarsfoundation.org/applicants/#programs

DuPont Challenge: http://thechallenge.dupont.com/essay/

Gates Millennium Scholars Program: http://www.gmsp.org/

General Electric: http://www.gefoundation.com/education/scholarships-programs/

National Eagle Scout Association: http://www.nesa.org/scholarships.html

National History Day Contest: http://www.nhd.org/contest-affiliates/

National Peace Day Contest: http://www.usip.org/category/course-type/national-peace-essay-contest

Prudential Spirit of Community Awards: http://spirit.prudential.com/view/page/soc/14830

Ronald McDonald House Charities: http://www.rmhc.org/rmhc-us-scholarships

Sallie Mae: https://www.salliemae.com/plan-for-college/scholarships/

Scholastic Art and Writing Awards: http://www.artandwriting.org/

Toshiba/NSTA Explora Vision Contest:
http://www.toshiba.com/csr/social_ed_eva.jsp

Tylenol:
http://www.tylenol.com/news/scholarship?id=tylenol/news/subptyschol.inc

Young Naturalist Awards: http://www.amnh.org/learn-teach/young-naturalist-awards

Student Loan Information

College and the Military: http://www.students.gov

General financial aid information: http://www.savingforcollege.com

Information on federal loans: https://studentaid.ed.gov/resources

Information on types of student loans:
http://www.debt.org/students/types-of-loans/

Internal Revenue Service: http://www.irs.gov

Loan repayment calculator: http://calculators.collegetoolkit.com/college-calculators/rescalcloan.aspx

Acknowledgements

A book is never the effort of one person. There are so many people that provided help, advice, guidance, and information along the way. This book would not have been complete without their help. Thank you first and foremost to all the admissions officers and deans that took the time to answer my questions. I'd also like to thank the countless students that shared with me their concerns, thoughts, and insight. Thank you to my friends and family for your unwavering support and encouragement.

To my wife, thank you for putting up with the long nights of me tapping away at the keys. I would also like to thank my teachers and professors for their dedication. Your contributions both to individuals and society are immeasurable.

About the Author

 Austin F. Fadely grew up a native of Southern Maryland and attended undergrad in Baltimore at UMBC, where he majored in English Communications with minors in History and Psychology. After spending several years as a textbook writer and editor, Austin moved to Winston-Salem, NC. Around that time, he shifted careers and became a project manager for software design and development.

Austin attended Wake Forest University, where he earned his MBA. In late 2014, Austin returned to the DC area to take up consulting. Austin currently lives in northern Virginia with his wife and three children.